Bank of Elon: IMF 2.0

Slava Solodkiy

Published by Slava Solodkiy, 2024.

While every precaution has been taken in the preparation of this book, the publisher assumes no responsibility for errors or omissions, or for damages resulting from the use of the information contained herein.

BANK OF ELON: IMF 2.0

First edition. December 11, 2024.

Copyright © 2024 Slava Solodkiy.

ISBN: 979-8230996071

Written by Slava Solodkiy.

Table of Contents

Table of Contents 5
I. Bank of Elon: Why Stop at Dollars? The Currency of Chaos 6
From Fed Challenger to Fed Creator: The Silicon Valley Fed? 7
The Risks of Revolution: The Future's Wild Card 8
II. The Grand Farce of Banking Governance: A 'Fintech' Satire in Three Acts 10
Act I: Captain Obvious and the Circus of Disjointed Regulators 11
Act II: The SVB Debacle, or How to Blame the Victim While Sounding Super Smart 12
Act III: The Regulators' Masquerade Ball—Everyone's Invited! 13
Epilogue: A Duct-Taped System in Need of a Real Overhaul 14
III. Rethinking the System: From SVB's Collapse to the Future of Money 18
SVB's Collapse as a Systemic Indicator: Regulatory and Structural Critique 21
Role of Innovation and Monoline Banks: International and Future Banking Systems 23
Role of Regulators: System Design, Future of Currency and Banking 25
IV. SVB Collapse and Regulatory Misalignment Analysis 30
1. The Maturity Risk Management Problem: 31
2. Regulatory and Policy Misalignment 32
3. The Complexity of Bank/Holding Company Structures 33
4. Avoiding the Harder Discussion on Crypto and Stablecoins 34
5. Lack of a Coherent, Long-Term Strategy by the Fed and Policymakers 35
V. Summers' Comments on Risk 37
1. Digital Banking, Easy Account Opening, and Deposit Mobility ... 38
2. Reexamining the Definitions of Current Accounts, Deposits, and Insurance 40

VI. Who Bears Responsibility: Client vs. Bank vs. Regulator 42
4. Inter-Banking Market Discipline and Subordinated Bonds 43
5. The Federal Reserve's Original Purpose and Modern Complexity.44
VII. SVB Collapse and Systemic Risk Insights.......................................46
1. Systemic Fragility and the Absence of Long-Term Vision 47
2. The Cross-Border Challenge: Beyond "Banking Groups"................48
3. International vs. Local Banks: Summaries Without Substance.......49
4. Full-Reserve and Narrow Banking: The Unanswered "What If?"..50
5. Rethinking the Private/Public Division of Labor in Risk 51
6. The "Monoliner" Concept and Systemic Diversity 53
7. Moving Beyond Summaries to Architecture 54
Regulatory Challenges and Systemic Fragility 56
1. The Absence of a Coherent National Strategy 57
2. Regulatory Inertia and Political Economy.......................................58
3. The Confusing Case of SVB and State-level Action 59
4. The Reluctance to Engage with Emerging Sectors: Crypto, Stablecoins, CBDC 60
5. The Need for a Strategic Vision and Architecture............................61
6. Toward a More Adaptive Regulatory Framework 62
Systemic Problems and Leadership Inaction..65
1. The Myth of Deliberate Design 66
2. The Danger of Retrospective Rationalization 67
3. The Limits of the Expert Mindset...68
4. Asking the Bigger "Why?"..69
5. The Broader Lesson: Beyond Banking..70
6. The Value of Fresh Perspectives and Interdisciplinary Thinking.....71
X. Monoliners and Systemic Risk: A Better Understanding.................73
1. Specialization vs. Homogenization 74
2. Systemic Resilience Through Diversity..75
3. Innovation Through Risk-Taking and Experimentation 76
4. Rethinking the Regulator's Role 77
5. Beyond the $250k Deposits Limit 78
6. The Big Picture: Stepping Beyond Captain Obvious 79

XI. The Fed, Rumors, and Bailout Economics 81
1. The Rumor-Driven Vulnerability and the Fed's Role 82
2. The Media-Savvy Client Base: Information Flows and Responsibility 83
3. The Government "Bailouts" That Make Money (Eventually) 84
4. "Privatized Gains, Socialized Losses"—Populist Rhetoric or Real Concern? 85
5. The Regulator's Role in Shaping Outcomes and Narratives 86
XII. Embracing the Reality of Our Fictions 89
1. The Illusion of Full Insurance 90
2. The Role of Psychological Comfort 91
3. The "Adult" vs. "Childish" Position 92
4. The Cost of Truth 93
5. The Humanist Perspective 94
The Question of Small and Medium-sized Banks vs. Mega-banks (or Monoliners vs. Specialized?) 96
1. The Idea of Direct Fed Accounts (Payment Infrastructure) 97
2. Monoliners and Specialized Banking Services 99
3. The Question of Small and Medium-Sized Banks vs. Mega-Banks 101
4. Finding a Balance 102
XIV. The Fed's Role in Systemic Stability 105
1. Political Clout and Status Quo Preservation 106
2. Revolutionaries Running Back to the Old System 107
3. SVB's "Failure" as a Mirror of the System 108
4. Rumors, Runs, and the Fed's Absence 109
5. SVB as a "Model Student" and the School's Failure 110
6. What's the Fed's Role and Plan? 111
XV. Financial System Reform and Central Bank Analysis 113
1. Stablecoins as a Transitional Proof-of-Concept to CBDCs and Cross-Border Monetary Infrastructure 114
2. The Confusing Hybrid of the U.S. Monetary System: Regulatory Complexity and Fragmentation 116

3. Roadblocks to Modernizing Infrastructure 118
XVI. The US Banking Sector's Historically Dependent Role 121
1. FDIC: From Insurer to De-Facto Regulator 122
2. FinCEN: The Stealth Enforcer 123
3. OCC: The Would-Be Modernizer Stymied by Lobbyists 124
4. A Confused, Layered Regulatory Ecosystem: Why Is It So Messed Up? 125
XVII. Separation of State as Owner, Regulator, and Client 129
1. Disaggregating the Central Bank's Roles 130
2. Encouraging More, Smaller Banks: Surplus or Shortage of Money 133
3. Focus on Real Outcomes, Not Just Profitability: Evolution, Not Revolution 134
XVIII. Reforming Central Bank Structure and Strategy 136
1. A Unified, Modern Infrastructure for Banking Ledgers 137
2. Clear and Transparent Regulatory Rules: A More Agile Regulatory Philosophy 138
3. Redefining the Fed's Functions and Strategy, Reforming the Fragmented U.S. Regulatory Landscape 139
4. Integrate Dollar and Bond Transparency: Compete Globally by Offering Infrastructure 141
XIX. A Revolution in Motion: Bridging Finance, Identity, and the Digital Frontier 144
Correspondent Banking: A Unique Opportunity for CBDCs and Digital Identity 147
The Untapped Potential of Correspondent Banking with CBDCs: The Future of Cross-Border Payments 148
Digital Identity: Enhancing Security and Compliance 149
XX. IMF 2.0: The SDR Strikes Back in a Multipolar Metaverse 151
Cambridge's and Oxford's Recent Case Studies 152
SDRs: From Dusty Relic to Digital Superstar 158
Multilateral Swap Lines 2.0: The IMF's Liquidity Lollipops 159
BRICS, Baskets, and the Rise of Regional Fintech Superheroes 160

China's Digital Yuan: The Death Star of the Old System? 161
Tech Giants: Beyond Borders, Beyond Baskets, Beyond Belief 162
XXI. A Blueprint for a Future Beyond the Fossilized Financial Order 164
Copy Before You Innovate: Reverse Engineering for the Ideal Use Case 165
Embrace the "Technical Debt" Concept and the Clean-Slate Reboot 167
Disruptive Innovation as a Political Strategy 168
Political Plans as MVPs and Experiments 169
Expanding "Political Imagination" Through Technology Mindsets 170
From Patchwork to Reinvention 171
Stablecoins as a Dress Rehearsal: Infrastructure as the New Currency 172
The Central Bank Autopsy: Unleashing a Wave of Competition 173
Embrace the Unknown and Evolve: The Coming Era of Global Financial Competition 175
The Grand Reset 176
P.S. The Bank of Elon: A Galactic Experiment in Monetary Tomfoolery 178
Elon Musk as a Policy Influencer and Public Figure 179
The "New Politician" Concept: Elon Musk's Political Influence 183
Media's Skepticism and the "Techno-Optimist" Mythos 185
Bank of Elon: A Galaxy-Brained Vision 187
Fed Reserve vs. Musk: Clash of the Eons 188
Re-Imagining SVB and the Financial Ecosystem: A New Role for the Dollar—Or Its Demise? 189
The Grand Theatre of Modern Finance: 'Electra' vs 'Libra' - Money as Votes 191

Bank of Elon: IMF 2.0
'SVB moment' for the Fed
'Bank of Elon': Reinventing the [X]USD
Larry Summers as a Reflection of the System
IMF 2.0: The Metaverse SDR Strikes Back

bank.run by Slava Solodkiy

E-book ISBN: 9798230926085 | **Print book ISBN:** 9798230996071

The collapse of **Silicon Valley Bank** (SVB) was not just another failure of a financial institution. It was a revelation, a crack in the mirror reflecting the fragility of the financial system and the complacency of its stewards. It wasn't just about poor management or a mismatched balance sheet—it was a systemic failure of vision, strategy, and accountability. And yet, as the dust settles, we have a unique opportunity to ask not just *what happened* but *what could be*.

Larry Summers, the Great Oracle of Finance, stepped into the spotlight with all the grace of an academic who hasn't sniffed reality in a few decades. He solemnly declares that the collapse of Silicon Valley Bank—some "piddly 16th largest bank" with the systemic importance of a mid-sized lemonade stand—represents a bigger deal than we ever realized.

Elon Musk has his sights set on revolutionizing finance: John Foley[1]'s recent FT article[2] delves into Musk's ambitious plan to transform his social network X into a full-fledged financial platform. This bold move, fueled by shifting regulations for industrial loan companies (ILCs), could unleash a wave of innovation in the banking sector, but not without potential perils. Foley explores the exciting possibilities—increased competition, groundbreaking financial products—alongside the looming risks to financial stability. Could 'Bank of Elon' become a reality? Foley suggests it's not as far-fetched as it sounds.

This isn't just a story about SVB (Summers or Musk). It's a story about us—our regulators, our banks, and the structures we've built. It's about how we've become obsessed with maintaining the *status quo*, how central banks like the Federal Reserve, born out of a visionary inter-bank agreement over a century ago, have morphed into reactionary institutions, always looking backward instead of forward.

BANK OF ELON: IMF 2.0

https://l.Nansen.id/**UnveilingEBook**   https://l.Nansen.id/**JusticeEBook**

- Larry Summers' Perspective on SVB: Symbolism of Summers as a Reflection of the System

- How SVB's Collapse Foretold the Fed's Reckoning

- The Rise of the 'Bank of Elon' and the X-End of the USD Empire

- Larry Summers: Portrait of an Empire in Decline

- IMF 2.0: The SDR Strikes Back in a Multipolar Metaverse

https://l.Nansen.id/**listenmeonSpotify**

I. Bank of Elon: Why Stop at Dollars? The Currency of Chaos

Elon Musk, the perennial disruptor of industries, stands poised at the precipice of financial innovation—or, depending on your perspective, financial chaos. What if the man who brought us flamethrowers, reusable rockets, and electric cars decides to reinvent banking? The "Bank of Elon" isn't just a financial institution—it's a revolution wrapped in a meme, designed to unsettle the foundations of the Federal Reserve itself.

After all, who better to challenge the entrenched guardians of global finance than the man who turned a social media platform into an "everything app"? X, Musk's ambitious reinvention of Twitter, is no longer just a playground for hot takes and cat videos—it's the embryonic stage of a financial empire.

Facebook's ill-fated Libra was a warning shot, a crude attempt to wade into the murky waters of monetary creation. It was smothered under the weight of political suspicion and regulatory disdain. Zuckerberg dared to dream, but Musk dares to *act*. He's already proven his ability to dance between the raindrops of regulation, from pushing the limits of SEC patience to launching satellites with impunity.

Imagine X, coupled with Starlink's global reach, Tesla's infrastructure, and SpaceX's penchant for the unimaginable. Why stop at competing with traditional banks? Musk could bypass them entirely. The "X Dollar" (or "MuskCoin," because branding is half the battle) might emerge as a decentralized currency backed by the sweat equity of Teslas and the orbital real estate of Starlink.

From Fed Challenger to Fed Creator: The Silicon Valley Fed?

Musk has a unique ace up his sleeve: access. His closeness to power brokers, his cultural cachet, and his ability to galvanize a legion of supporters could align in ways that even the Federal Reserve might fear. While Zuck's Libra floundered under the scrutiny of regulators terrified of tech-induced monetary destabilization, Musk operates with a reckless audacity that makes him less a businessman and more a mythic figure in the halls of innovation.

Let's imagine the unimaginable: a partnership with a Trump-esque administration, eager to decentralize traditional power structures, eager to stick it to Wall Street. With regulatory barriers eased, the X ecosystem could transform into a financial juggernaut, blending digital payments, loans, and investments with the seamless efficiency of Tesla's autopilot.

Elon's history with PayPal provides a precedent, but his ambitions surely extend beyond mere payments. He could reimagine the very role of central banking. The X Bank wouldn't just take deposits; it might offer investment in space exploration or renewable energy as a default savings plan. Interest? Paid in kilowatt-hours, redeemable at Tesla charging stations. Loans? Collateralized by your FSD-enabled Model 3.

And while the Federal Reserve frets over inflation and interest rates, Elon's "MuskCoin" could tether its value to something tangible—say, the output of Tesla factories or the orbital slots controlled by SpaceX. Forget the gold standard; welcome to the "Gigafactory standard."

The Risks of Revolution: The Future's Wild Card

Yet, the risks are monumental. Banking isn't just about innovation—it's about trust. The FDIC, already leery of tech giants dabbling in finance, would likely balk at Musk's penchant for upending convention. The specter of systemic risk looms large. Imagine a financial crash triggered not by subprime mortgages, but by a glitch in Tesla's operating system or a mass exodus of users from X.

Moreover, Musk's tendency to alienate and antagonize could spell doom. Banking is a realm where confidence is currency. A stray tweet could vaporize billions in seconds—a prospect that even the most diehard "Elonites" might struggle to accept.

"Bank of Elon" is a tantalizing, terrifying prospect. It's the marriage of Silicon Valley audacity with Wall Street gravity. It could redefine financial systems—or destroy them. But if anyone's going to reinvent the rules of the game, it's Elon Musk. Because when the world is a gameboard, and you're playing for Mars, who cares if a few central banks tremble along the way?

II. The Grand Farce of Banking Governance: A 'Fintech' Satire in Three Acts

Picture this: Larry Summers, the Great Oracle of Finance, stepping into the spotlight with all the grace of an academic who hasn't sniffed reality in a few decades. He solemnly declares that the collapse of Silicon Valley Bank—some "piddly 16th largest bank" with the systemic importance of a mid-sized lemonade stand—represents a bigger deal than we ever realized. Isn't it precious how this sounds both profound and meaningless at the same time? Bravo, Larry. Truly, a performance worthy of the world's smallest violin.

Act I: Captain Obvious and the Circus of Disjointed Regulators

Summers rattles off a list of pearls: US Treasury does one thing, the Federal Reserve does another, and they "surprisingly" don't coordinate. The market flutters its eyelashes and pretends to be shocked, shocked I say! Because in what sane universe do two big, old, cranky bureaucracies happily skip hand-in-hand? Next, he treats us to a classic #CaptainObvious line: "Maybe, just maybe, we need to think more carefully about regulating banks and their holding companies." Wow, stop the presses. In other news, water is wet.

Meanwhile, the regulators—Fed, Treasury, FDIC, OCC, FinCEN—are all performing their own interpretive dances of oversight. Each claims unique superpowers but often cancels each other out in a tangle of contradictory mandates and century-old byzantine rules. It's like watching an orchestra where the violinist plays death metal, the flutist wants EDM, and the drummer's on strike because the others won't play that Bach sonata backwards. The result? A big, off-key mess. But hey, at least it's "stable," right?

Act II: The SVB Debacle, or How to Blame the Victim While Sounding Super Smart

Summer's commentary on SVB's collapse: "Opening a bank that takes short-term deposits and invests them long-term is dumb." Oh my, such insight! Next he'll tell us that putting your hand in a fire burns. Except, dear Larry, wasn't that the entire premise of modern banking for, oh, a century or two? Maturity transformation is the bread and butter of these institutions—until it isn't. And when it isn't, apparently it's news. SVB had no grand strategy. It was complacent, lazy, and coasting on the Silicon Valley hype. Shocker. Then, when they stumbled, people screamed: "Where was the Fed?" Indeed, where was our mighty central bank, that gallant knight sworn to slay liquidity dragons and keep rumor-driven panic at bay? Turns out the Fed's role is mostly to stand in the corner like a bashful teenager at prom, refusing to dance. Why would it stop a systemic panic when it could simply wag its finger afterward, saying, "I told you so" (even if it didn't)?

Act III: The Regulators' Masquerade Ball—Everyone's Invited!

Summers (and all the rest of these dignified sages) pretend that the current system was handed down on stone tablets by the gods of finance. Truth is, it's a patchwork of historical accidents and half-baked compromises. Imagine the Constitution of banking was drafted during a drunken frat party in 1917 and has only been amended by adding sticky notes in the margins for a hundred years. The result? Regulators tripping over each other's feet, bank holding companies that can't hold anything but confusion, and the Fed peeking out the window like a paranoid landlord who's rented rooms to a bunch of circus clowns.

And let's not forget those pesky critics who say "privatized gains and socialized losses" are bad. Summers and friends scoff at them: "How dare you, simpleton! Don't you know that when we bail out the banks, we eventually make a profit for the taxpayer? Someday... maybe... if you just wait a few decades and squint really hard." This is apparently the financial equivalent of buying avocado futures—surely it'll pay off once the market recovers and millennials start making guacamole again.

We also get the joy of hearing about how customers, who have long been sold the fairy tale that "your money is safe, trust us," suddenly aren't responsible for performing forensic audits on their bank's balance sheets. The nerve! Didn't everyone major in advanced bank risk management in high school? This must be news to the expert pundits who think shifting blame onto depositors is easier than rethinking the rotten system underneath.

Epilogue: A Duct-Taped System in Need of a Real Overhaul

In the grand finale, Summers and his compatriots fail to ask the real question: Why are we still driving this old jalopy of a financial system, souped up with duct-tape and gadgetry from the 1920s and expecting it to handle warp speed in 2023? Instead, we get polite nods to "revisiting fundamentals" and "rethinking maturity risk," and maybe a hint that we need more "international consideration." Yawn.

Let's be honest, the SVB collapse and all these oh-so-wise postmortems highlight one thing: Our entire financial regulatory apparatus is a Dr. Frankenstein creation. We keep shoving on more body parts—CBDCs! Stablecoins! Special purpose charters!—and marvel when the monster lurches off into the night. The regulators remain too busy patting themselves on the back for "not being worse" to consider that maybe it's time to rebuild from scratch.

So yes, SVB is a canary, not just in a coal mine but in a labyrinth of tangled pipes, moldy old wiring, and suspicious smells. The Summers sermon reminds us that our wise elders are still stuck playing yesterday's tunes on broken instruments. Until someone steps up to hack away at the thicket of #StatusQuo, we'll keep pretending to be shocked when the next bank topples over. And the experts? They'll keep telling us what we "should have" known, after the fact, through a haze of hindsight and pseudo-wisdom. Cue the applause, and goodnight.

These notes raise significant questions about the direction of global banking systems, the role of central regulators, and the future interplay between traditional and innovative financial models. It emphasizes the importance of systemic reevaluation over piecemeal solutions, advocating for a thoughtful, strategic approach to finance in an evolving world.

These thoughts were inspired by interviews[3] of **Larry Summers**[4], a prominent economist and former U.S. Treasury Secretary, in relation to his comments[5] on the collapse of Silicon Valley Bank (SVB):

- Summers' focus on general and well-known points about risk management and regulatory misalignment is perceived as superficial and lacking depth.

- While he identifies some valid systemic issues, the critique suggests that he fails to provide detailed solutions or meaningful insights.

- Summers' tendency to comment on systemic issues with a "Captain Obvious" approach—stating problems without delving into their roots or offering actionable recommendations.

- His discussions are seen as retrospective and focused on preserving the status quo rather than pushing forward-thinking solutions.

- Summers as a symbol of broader systemic problems within the financial regulatory and intellectual elite: the reliance on outdated paradigms, the lack of innovation, and a failure to ask fundamental questions about systemic architecture.

- His commentary represents the limits of "expert" analysis when detached from practical, entrepreneurial, or forward-thinking perspectives.

- Summers' outlook is paralleled with the broader failure of the Federal Reserve and other regulators to adapt to modern financial realities. His remarks are seen as indicative of a system focused more on managing symptoms than addressing root causes.

Summers' mention serves as a focal point to explore deeper critiques of the banking and regulatory systems, positioning him as both a commentator on the SVB crisis and a stand-in for the intellectual inertia of the financial establishment.

III. Rethinking the System: From SVB's Collapse to the Future of Money

- **SVB as a Reflection of the System**: SVB's failure is less about its management and more about systemic weaknesses mirrored across the industry.

- **Fed's Dual Identity**: The Fed as both a reactionary body and a Siamese twin of the Treasury creates inherent conflicts in policy and accountability.

- **Innovation's Double-Edged Sword**: The tension between systemic risk from monoline innovations and the stagnation of universal banking models.

- **Consumer Expectations vs. Reality**: The unrealistic demand for absolute safety in deposits contrasts with the inherent risk in any insurance model.

At the heart of the SVB story lies a striking irony. Here was a bank, celebrated as the financial backbone of Silicon Valley, a hub of innovation, yet utterly devoid of innovation in its own strategy. For years, it drifted along, parasitizing on the growth of the tech sector, avoiding hard questions about its purpose and future. When trouble hit—a combination of concentrated risk, regulatory gaps, and sheer rumor—the entire system wobbled. If the 16th largest bank in the U.S., with less than 1% of system-wide assets, could send shockwaves through the economy, doesn't that reveal something deeply flawed about the system itself?

But this isn't just a story about SVB. It's a story about us—our regulators, our banks, and the structures we've built. It's about how we've become obsessed with maintaining the *status quo*, clinging to outdated systems while the world changes around us. It's about how central banks like the Federal Reserve, born out of a visionary inter-bank agreement over a century ago, have morphed into reactionary institutions, always looking backward instead of forward.

The Fed, with its patchwork DNA of regional compromises and competing mandates, has become the epitome of institutional inertia. Created as an interbank platform to stabilize liquidity, it now struggles to reconcile its multiple identities: a lender, a regulator, a payments facilitator, and a symbol of monetary trust. Its tools are outdated, its vision unclear. It reacts to crises with ad hoc measures but offers no strategy for the future.

What should the future look like? For one, it's time to question the very architecture of our financial system. Why do we still rely on composite balance sheets that mix short-term liabilities with long-term assets, creating systemic fragility? Why does the Fed play the role of a reluctant firefighter, stepping in only when the house is already ablaze? Why haven't we built a real-time, transparent system where every bank's risks and reserves are visible, not just to regulators but to the public?

Imagine a different world. In this world, every account is directly mirrored in a central ledger, accessible to regulators in real time. Banks are no longer conglomerates trying to do everything for everyone; instead, they specialize, becoming lean, focused monoliners. Stablecoins and Central Bank Digital Currencies (CBDCs) coexist, each playing to its strengths: stablecoins providing user-friendly interfaces and niche services, while CBDCs offer stability and trust. Interoperability between these forms of money is seamless, allowing consumers and businesses to switch between them effortlessly.

In this future, regulators are not passive observers but active architects. They recognize that innovation often comes from the fringes—from fintech startups, from monoline banks willing to take risks, from technologies like blockchain. Instead of stifling these innovations with one-size-fits-all rules, they create flexible frameworks that encourage experimentation while managing risks. They understand that their role is not just to regulate but to enable, to act as arbiters of liquidity, to stabilize without stifling.

And then there's the big question: the role of money itself. Today, the U.S. dollar is as much a system of infrastructure as it is a currency, underpinning global trade and finance. But this dominance is being challenged—not just by rivals like China but by the very nature of financial innovation. The future of money may not be about currencies at all. It may be about infrastructure: the platforms, protocols, and systems that allow value to flow. In this future, the Fed and other central banks must evolve or risk irrelevance.

SVB's Collapse as a Systemic Indicator: Regulatory and Structural Critique

The collapse of Silicon Valley Bank (SVB) was not just another failure of a financial institution. It was a revelation, a crack in the mirror reflecting the fragility of the financial system and the complacency of its stewards.

- The SVB crisis exposed broader structural flaws in the financial system rather than being an isolated failure.

- Issues like mismatched regulatory strategies between the U.S. Treasury and Federal Reserve, and the lack of long-term strategy in both the bank (SVB) and the regulators.

- The U.S. banking system and regulatory environment lack cohesion, with fragmented oversight among state, federal, and specialized regulators like the FDIC and OCC.

- The Federal Reserve's reactionary approach and lack of strategic vision for the next 5-10 years.

- The reliance on "composite balances" (short-term deposits funding long-term investments) highlights systemic vulnerabilities.

- Debate on the role of central banks, including suggestions for transitioning to full-reserve banking[6] or rethinking the Fed's function.

- Overlap and conflicts among U.S. banking regulators dilute accountability and efficacy.

- Resistance to modernization (e.g., delayed implementation of FedNow) due to entrenched interests of regional banks.

- The Fed's inconsistent response to bank crises undermines trust in the system's stability.

- Perception of favoring entrenched banking players over new fintech entrants or societal interests.

- Debate on whether to shield consumers from financial risks or allow greater transparency and responsibility.

- Influence of regional banks and state regulators in national banking policy hinders progress and adaptability.

Role of Innovation and Monoline Banks: International and Future Banking Systems

It wasn't just about poor management or a mismatched balance sheet—it was a systemic failure of vision, strategy, and accountability. And yet, as the dust settles, we have a unique opportunity to ask not just *what happened* but *what could be*.

- Monoline banks (focused on niche markets) are critical for systemic innovation but come with heightened individual risk.

- Centralized approaches, such as mega-banks or state-dominated systems like Canada's, stifle competition and innovation.

- Predictions about the rise of international banking institutions over localized systems.

- Infrastructure (e.g., CBDCs, cross-border banking arrangements) becoming the new "currency."

- Complexity in account types (checking, savings, term deposits) creates confusion for consumers.

- Calls for simplified financial products with transparent risk communication.

- **Infrastructure as Currency**: Predicts a shift from traditional fiat currencies to infrastructure-driven monetary systems (e.g., CBDCs enabling cross-border direct lending).

- **Monoline Dominance**: Advocates for a future banking landscape dominated by specialized, niche-focused banks rather than universal banks.

- **New Inter-Bank Arrangements**: Foresees the potential replacement of existing central banking models with more dynamic, global inter-bank systems.

- **Evolution of Deposit Insurance**: Calls for a reimagining of deposit insurance mechanisms, acknowledging their psychological and systemic nature rather than economic absoluteness.

Role of Regulators: System Design, Future of Currency and Banking

The collapse of Silicon Valley Bank (SVB) has sent shockwaves through the financial world, but its implications extend far beyond the immediate fallout. This event has exposed critical vulnerabilities in the financial system and raises profound questions about the role of regulators, the future of banking, and the very nature of money itself.

- Should regulators act as passive observers or active risk mitigators in systemic crises?

- How can regulators balance fostering innovation while maintaining systemic stability?

- Are current banking architectures and composite balance norms sustainable, or is a shift to full-reserve or narrow banking inevitable?

- To what extent should consumers be informed of risks, and how much responsibility should they bear for financial decisions?

- What role will central banks play in a world where infrastructure might replace traditional currency as a medium of exchange?

One of the key issues highlighted by SVB's failure is the mismatch between the short-term nature of deposits and the long-term nature of assets. This imbalance, coupled with a lack of diversification in SVB's portfolio, created a liquidity crisis when interest rates rose. The Federal Reserve's actions, while intended to stabilize the situation, have also revealed a concerning lack of coordination among regulators.

The traditional banking model, where banks take short-term deposits and invest in long-term assets, is being challenged by the rise of digital banking and new financial technologies. The lines between different types of accounts and financial products are blurring, and the regulatory framework has struggled to keep up.

The SVB case also raises questions about the role of the Federal Reserve in overseeing the banking system. Is the Fed fulfilling its role as an arbiter of liquidity, or has it become a reactive and outdated institution? The Fed's lack of a clear strategy and its reliance on outdated systems and processes are a cause for concern.

The rise of stablecoins and central bank digital currencies (CBDCs) further complicates the picture. These new forms of digital money have the potential to disrupt the traditional banking system and challenge the role of central banks. The Fed's reluctance to engage with these developments is troubling, as it suggests a desire to protect the status quo rather than embrace innovation.

The SVB collapse has also exposed the limitations of expertise and the dangers of relying on past experience in a rapidly changing world. Experts often fail to see the bigger picture and are reluctant to challenge their own assumptions.

The concentration of risk in certain banks and the potential for rumors to trigger bank runs are further challenges that need to be addressed. The role of the Fed in mitigating these risks is unclear, and its actions during the SVB crisis have raised more questions than answers.

The idea of privatized gains and socialized losses has also come into focus, with questions about the fairness of government bailouts and the need for greater transparency and accountability in the financial system.

The concept of a "direct Fed account for everyone" has been proposed as a way to separate checking and savings accounts and provide greater stability to the system. This idea, while intriguing, raises questions about the role of banks and the potential for government overreach.

The SVB case has also highlighted the challenges faced by small and medium-sized banks in competing with larger institutions. The role of regional banks in the U.S. banking system is being questioned, as is the Fed's ability to foster innovation and competition.

The collapse of SVB is a wake-up call for the financial industry and its regulators: It is time to rethink the fundamental principles of banking, embrace innovation, and create a more resilient and inclusive financial system for the future. The Fed must step up and fulfill its role as a leader and innovator, or risk being left behind in a rapidly changing world.

- The collapse of SVB highlights systemic issues within the Federal Reserve (Fed) and the banking sector, particularly a lack of clear strategy and focus on maintaining the status quo rather than innovation and addressing real problems.

- The Fed's response to the SVB crisis indicates a lack of understanding of the evolving banking landscape and the role of new technologies like stablecoins and CBDCs.

- There is a need for clearer regulation and guidelines regarding the banking sector, especially concerning the responsibilities of banks and the government in managing risk.

- The Fed's lack of a clear strategy and focus on short-term goals hinders the development and competitiveness of the US banking sector.

- The current regulatory framework is complex and outdated, with multiple agencies having overlapping responsibilities, leading to confusion and potential conflicts.

- The concentration of power in regional banks with limited vision and strong political influence prevents necessary reforms and progress.

- The concept of "infrastructure as a new currency" where the infrastructure for issuing and circulating liabilities becomes more important than traditional currencies.

- The rise of international banking institutions and new inter-bank agreements that could potentially challenge the dominance of national central banks.

- Rethinking the role of banks, including the separation of core banking functions from other financial services and the potential for direct Fed accounts for everyone.

- What is the role of the Fed in the current banking system, and how should it evolve to address future challenges?

- How can the regulatory framework be simplified and made more transparent to foster innovation and competition while ensuring stability?

- What is the future of money and banking in a world increasingly shaped by technology and globalization?

- Viewing the SVB collapse as a reflection of the Fed's own shortcomings rather than solely blaming the bank's management.

- Emphasizing the importance of "mono-liners" (banks specializing in specific niches) for the overall health and development of the banking system.

- Challenging the popular narrative of "privatized gains and socialized losses" and highlighting the potential for the government to profit from market interventions.

The SVB collapse was a wake-up call, but it's not too late: The financial system doesn't need another round of patchwork fixes. It needs a revolution—or at least a bold evolution. We must rethink the role of banks, the structure of regulation, and the very nature of money. The choice is ours: cling to the *status quo* or embrace a future that is more transparent, inclusive, and resilient. This isn't just about fixing what's broken. It's about imagining what could be—and having the courage to build it.

IV. SVB Collapse and Regulatory Misalignment Analysis

It's understandable why the recent failure of Silicon Valley Bank (SVB) set off a broad wave of discussion—not just among the media and market watchers, but also among high-level policymakers and thought leaders like Larry Summers. Although much of the mainstream conversation has focused on the immediate, surface-level issues (rapid deposit outflows, misalignment of asset/liability duration, a fragile depositor base), Summers' commentary and similar critiques are attempting to point out that the SVB collapse may be symptomatic of more systemic, deeply-rooted issues within the U.S. financial and regulatory system. Let's unpack some of the points you raised, as well as some underlying themes.

1. The Maturity Risk Management Problem:

Summers and others have emphasized the mismatch between short-term liabilities (like demand deposits) and longer-term assets (like bonds or loans). SVB was a rather extreme example: it took in huge amounts of short-term deposits from a concentrated client base (tech startups and venture funds) during an era of near-zero interest rates, and then invested heavily in longer-dated securities. When interest rates rose, the value of those securities fell, and a subsequent confidence crisis triggered depositors to flee. On a basic level, yes, "opening a bank that takes deposits short to buy bonds long" is risky. But if we peel back the layers, the real point is that in the current era of modern banking, nearly every institution is playing a certain degree of this maturity transformation game—it's essentially baked into traditional commercial banking. The problem highlighted by SVB isn't new, but it shows that the tools and models banks use to manage interest rate and duration risk must evolve. The old assumptions—like an extended low-rate environment—no longer hold.

2. Regulatory and Policy Misalignment

A particularly resonant theme is that different arms of the U.S. economic governance system—Treasury, the Fed, various bank regulators—operate on their own timelines, with their own policy horizons and objectives, sometimes with insufficient coordination. Summers suggests that we have a problem when, for example, the Federal Reserve tightens monetary policy aggressively (rapid rate hikes) while the Treasury and other regulators haven't fully adapted their frameworks to the new reality. This mismatch can cause unexpected market sparks, as he puts it. What we see is a financial system that's sensitive to even small shocks, partly because no single regulator or policymaker is fully considering how their moves interplay with those of others. Each is operating with a siloed perspective, and financial institutions get caught in the crossfire.

3. The Complexity of Bank/Holding Company Structures

The arrangement of a bank and its holding company is not just a legal or corporate governance quirk; it defines what can be capitalized on a balance sheet, what is considered a core banking asset, and how profits and investments flow. Current regulations force a rigid separation:

- The bank entity itself must remain profitable under strict definitions and can generally only hold "bank-eligible" assets.

- Intellectual property, software, and other intangible long-term value drivers get pushed onto the holding company.

This structural separation can lead to perverse incentives, where the bank is constrained to optimize short-term, easily classifiable assets—often pushing it toward a maturity transformation model that may not be sustainable in a rising-rate environment. Summers highlights that we need to look more closely at these artificial silos, but what's missing from the regulatory discourse is a willingness to fundamentally reconsider how we structure and treat banks versus their parent entities. Without that, we'll see repeated cycles of risky balance-sheet maneuvers and belated attempts to fix them.

4. Avoiding the Harder Discussion on Crypto and Stablecoins

Summers (and many others in similar positions) often sidestepped discussions around crypto, stablecoins, and CBDCs. This avoidance might reflect not just a lack of deep familiarity, but also a reluctance to engage with a space that doesn't neatly fit into existing regulatory paradigms. The U.S. banking framework is still designed around traditional financial products, and the rapid evolution of digital assets challenges that framework. If regulators aren't up-to-speed or aren't willing to address these innovations, risk management deficiencies related to these new products could go unnoticed. The SVB situation touched on these assets indirectly (through customer portfolios, fintech partners, etc.), but the absence of candid discussion points to a knowledge gap at the regulatory level.

5. Lack of a Coherent, Long-Term Strategy by the Fed and Policymakers

One of my central concerns is the long-term direction of U.S. monetary policy and financial regulation. The argument that recent interventions—such as actions taken during the COVID crisis—were more ad hoc than strategic resonates. For the past 15 years (since at least the 2008 financial crisis), the Fed has largely been in perpetual "firefighting" mode, responding to crises with extraordinary tools. Quantitative easing, near-zero interest rates, and then a sudden pivot to tightening suggests a kind of improvisational approach rather than a steady, well-communicated, long-term vision.

This lack of a stable, forward-looking strategy leaves the financial system constantly guessing, and banks like SVB (and their depositors) often make decisions based on assumptions of continuity that can suddenly be undermined. When the environment changes abruptly—like a rapid series of rate hikes—institutions that haven't prepared for a less accommodative environment get caught off-guard. The problem isn't just mismanagement at an individual bank; it's also the absence of a clear, consistent roadmap from the nation's monetary authorities.

The collapse of SVB may appear as just a single bank failure caused by poor risk management and a panicky depositor base. But Summers and others hint at something deeper: a system that's structurally misaligned—where regulations encourage short-termism, where policymakers operate in their own silos, and where there is no coherent, forward-looking strategy guiding monetary and regulatory policy. This event is a signal that we must rethink how modern banking interacts with technology, liquidity, risk management, and a shifting macroeconomic landscape.

The SVB incident is thus more of a symptom than a one-off problem. It prompts us to ask: Are we willing to engage in a fundamental re-examination of how we regulate, supervise, and envision the banking sector and monetary policy? Or will we once again enact short-term fixes until the next spark ignites another crisis? The uneasy feeling here is that without structural changes, the system remains fragile, and SVB's downfall may be remembered as not just one mismanaged bank, but an early warning of deeper systemic vulnerabilities.

V. Summers' Comments on Risk

He often gestures toward crucial underlying issues without fully unpacking them. Let's break down some of these tangential points to see what might lie beneath and why they matter.

1. Digital Banking, Easy Account Opening, and Deposit Mobility

Summers mentions that modern, digital-first banking makes it much easier for customers to open multiple bank accounts and move their funds around quickly. On the surface, this sounds like a standard observation about "fintech" innovation. But what might he really be getting at?

- **Liquidity Flight:** In an age where a depositor can transfer millions at the tap of a smartphone, deposit bases are more fluid and less "sticky." This increases the volatility of bank liabilities. In the SVB case, once trust eroded, money left in a matter of hours. If regulators or bank risk managers are using models based on slower-moving, brick-and-mortar era deposit flows, those models need updating.

- **Competition and Concentration:** If customers can quickly open accounts at multiple banks, no single institution can easily force exclusivity. SVB was accused of pushing clients to keep all their funds there, possibly to stabilize its own liquidity metrics. If regulators now insist on enforcing a more open system—where such constraints can't exist—then competition could improve. Depositors would be less "locked in," and that might encourage banks to manage risk more prudently, knowing customers can leave at a moment's notice.

- **Deposit Insurance and Product Clarity:** Quick, frictionless account-hopping also puts pressure on the FDIC deposit insurance framework. If clients spread money across multiple banks for safety, the very architecture of deposit guarantees (caps per depositor per institution) might need rethinking. Are current insurance limits still appropriate in a world where one can open multiple accounts instantly?

2. Reexamining the Definitions of Current Accounts, Deposits, and Insurance

Summers suggests we need to revisit what we mean by deposits, insured balances, and various account types. This is crucial but often glossed over:

- **Client Confusion and Financial Literacy:** Many customers don't know the difference between a checking account, a savings account, a money market account, or a time deposit beyond superficial features. Likewise, terms like "insured funds" and "uninsured deposits" remain murky. The SVB scenario highlighted that many startups had millions parked in a single bank—money that often exceeded FDIC insurance limits—without fully appreciating their exposure to loss if the bank failed. If people can't make sense of these products and the associated risks, the system relies too heavily on implicit assumptions of safety.

- **Regulatory Clarity and Uniform Standards:** Banks sometimes bundle products and shift money internally between accounts in ways that blur risk boundaries. We need simpler, more transparent categories so both clients and regulators know what's what. Each product type (current account vs. custodial account vs. term deposit) should come with a clear risk profile, reporting standards, and insurance coverage. Without such clarity, panic-driven bank runs might happen more frequently and more violently.

3. Who Bears Responsibility: Client vs. Bank vs. Regulator

Summers' point that no client—be it a household or a tech startup—is truly equipped or obligated to perform in-depth due diligence on their bank is profound. This touches on a bigger philosophical and policy question:

- **Division of Labor in Risk Assessment:** We don't expect a restaurant patron to ensure the kitchen is up to health code; we have inspectors for that. Similarly, why should a depositor be expected to analyze a bank's duration risk, capital ratios, or management quality? Deposit insurance and bank regulation were invented precisely because most people can't and won't perform that analysis. If the system expects customers to be the first line of defense, it's setting them up for failure.

- **Scope of Government and Regulatory Intervention:** The government and its agencies (FDIC, Federal Reserve, state regulators) exist in part to ensure a stable financial environment so individuals and businesses can place their money in banks without living in constant fear of sudden losses. Reaffirming that responsibility may mean tighter supervision, more explicit standards, and clearer communication so that customers aren't left guessing about the safety of their funds.

4. Inter-Banking Market Discipline and Subordinated Bonds

Summers hints at the idea that the inter-bank lending markets could be reformed so that banks hold more risk-bearing instruments from each other (like subordinated debt). It's a tantalizing concept that he doesn't elaborate on, but we can guess the logic:

- **Skin in the Game for Banks:** If banks lend to each other not just through secured short-term loans but also through instruments that absorb losses (like subordinated bonds), then each bank has a vested interest in monitoring the solvency and risk-taking behaviors of its counterparties. This could create a self-policing system where banks limit each other's recklessness because no one wants to invest in a risky peer.

- **Market-Based Regulation:** Such market discipline could supplement (not replace) formal regulation. Instead of relying solely on government oversight, the banking community itself would have financial incentives to discourage imprudent practices. But for this to work, the instruments and markets must be well-designed, and regulators must ensure transparency and prevent hidden collusion or opaque risk-sharing that just shifts systemic risk around.

5. The Federal Reserve's Original Purpose and Modern Complexity

The Federal Reserve was created as a backstop to provide liquidity and prevent bank runs, stemming from lessons learned before the central bank's establishment in 1913 (the Federal Reserve Act was enacted in 1913, and the system began operations in 1914). Back then, the logic was simpler: banks needed a lender of last resort to curb panics. Over a century later, the system is vastly more complex:

- **Are We Still True to the Original Mission?**

    The Fed's role has expanded dramatically: it now manages monetary policy, ensures financial stability, and regulates banks. Each crisis (the Depression, the S&L crisis, the 2008 crisis, the COVID crisis) added layers of policy tools and new mandates. Maybe Summers is subtly calling attention to the drift from the original purpose. If we're essentially "taping batteries to a gasoline car," as you put it, then perhaps a complete re-architecture is needed. Instead of layering new rules on top of old logic, we might need to define a new foundational logic suited for digital banking, global financial integration, and rapid capital flows.

- **Back to Basics:** Rethinking what the Fed and other regulators are supposed to do might involve stripping away the accreted complexity and starting from first principles. Why do we have a central bank? To ensure liquidity and stability. Are the tools and regulatory frameworks we have today actually serving that end? If not, how can we reorganize and modernize the system so that it's coherent and resilient, rather than a patchwork of legacy rules and ad-hoc fixes?

Summers often points to critical issues—digital liquidity shifts, product category confusion, misaligned responsibilities, inter-bank discipline, and the Fed's original mission—yet fails to flesh them out. When fully elaborated, these points suggest the need for a fundamental rethinking of banking regulation and structure. Instead of piling on quick fixes, the call is for a more foundational approach: re-clarifying the roles of customers, banks, regulators, and the Federal Reserve itself; restructuring product definitions and insurance schemes; and ensuring that the tools and architectures in place align with our modern, digital financial reality.

Without going "back to basics" and re-evaluating the entire system's logic, all these incremental changes resemble patchwork solutions. Summers might only hint at these truths, but the subtext is that our current financial framework is outdated—and we need a more holistic and forward-looking redesign.

VII. SVB Collapse and Systemic Risk Insights

A crucial frustration: figures like Summers hint at systemic issues but rarely offer the granularity needed to turn big-picture critique into actionable insight. It's as if they're naming the chapters in a book without ever writing the content. Let's try to fill in some of those gaps and connect the dots.

1. Systemic Fragility and the Absence of Long-Term Vision

Summers' line —"if the fall of the 16th largest bank... causes the system to wobble"—is a loaded statement. It suggests a fundamental fragility in the financial system. But more deeply, it reveals a leadership class that has drifted from the original architectural logic of banking and monetary policy. If the system was built to withstand precisely these kinds of shocks (or at least smaller institutions folding without catastrophic ripple effects), and now it can't, what changed? The underlying problem is that the custodians of the system—central bankers, regulators, policy experts—often operate as incremental managers, not systemic architects. They know how to maintain the machine in its current form but have lost touch with why the machine was built this way in the first place, or what it might need to look like for the future.

This status-quo maintenance is not just institutional inertia; it's personal too. Thought leaders and policymakers benefit from being seen as stable hands, even if that stability is illusory. They prefer to patch the old logic rather than risk their reputations by calling for a root-and-branch redesign.

2. The Cross-Border Challenge: Beyond "Banking Groups"

Summers notes that banking groups in each country should be regulated as separate entities. On the surface, this is sensible and widely agreed upon. Yet this approach is too simplistic for today's interconnected world. Gone are the days when a bank's boundaries were strictly local. Modern banks are complex webs of subsidiaries, branches, and correspondent relationships spanning multiple jurisdictions. Problems arise when these entities shift risk and liquidity across borders, making it hard for any single regulator to grasp the true picture.

Real innovation would mean discussing how to build coherent global standards or frameworks that recognize the transnational nature of banking—something akin to a global rulebook or at least more robust cross-border supervisory colleges that share real-time data, harmonize risk assessments, and coordinate interventions. Instead of just calling them "banking groups" and stating the obvious need for separate local regulation, we need detailed proposals for how national regulators can cooperate (or even pool sovereignty in certain oversight areas) to reflect the global reality.

3. International vs. Local Banks: Summaries Without Substance

When Summers says that we'll see more international banking institutions, that's not exactly a revelation—financial globalization has been a trend for decades. The real question is: what regulatory, structural, and risk management frameworks do we need to handle that? How do we ensure stability when capital can move at the speed of light across borders, and systemic risks can arise from opaque global linkages?

Instead of just forecasting a world with more international banks, we need the "how" and "why." How do we harmonize deposit insurance regimes internationally? How do we handle bank resolution when a global bank fails in multiple jurisdictions simultaneously? Without that detail, it's just stating the obvious trend without grappling with the ramifications.

4. Full-Reserve and Narrow Banking: The Unanswered "What If?"

Summers raises the idea of full-reserve or narrow banking, then doesn't pursue it. This is a huge missed opportunity. Full-reserve banking, for instance, is a radically different approach to handling maturity transformation. Instead of allowing banks to lend out a large portion of deposits, full-reserve systems force banks to hold an equal amount of reserves for every deposit—essentially eliminating the classic run scenario. Similarly, "narrow banking" suggests that deposits should be fully matched by safe, short-term assets, while riskier lending happens elsewhere, funded by non-deposit instruments.

But these aren't just theoretical ideas; they challenge the very structure of modern banking. Moving toward such systems would mean re-defining the role of banks, possibly reducing the need for central bank backstops, and fundamentally altering the credit creation process. Without details, we're stuck with a tantalizing concept that never reaches practical exploration. Is such a system scalable? Would it hamper economic growth? Could technology (like stablecoins or CBDCs) facilitate a form of narrow banking at scale?

5. Rethinking the Private/Public Division of Labor in Risk

Summers returns to maturity transformation and implies that we need clearer boundaries between what is a private-sector risk and what is assumed by the state. He suggests that banks could handle shorter-horizon risks while the state manages longer-horizon systemic risks. But this simplistic division raises more questions than it answers:

- **The Nature of Risk:** How do we define "short," "medium," and "long" horizons in a complex, global economy where technology accelerates liquidity movements?

- **The Role of the Central Bank:** If the central bank (as part of the state) is the ultimate backstop, how do we prevent moral hazard while ensuring liquidity in crises?

- **Allocating Responsibility:** When a bank like SVB fails due to mismanagement, is it purely a private failure, or does it reflect a systemic design flaw that the regulator should have prevented? Summers hints that risk tolerance at the micro level (an individual bank) might reduce macro-level risks by not pushing everyone to the same low-risk, homogeneous model. This idea is fascinating: a diverse ecosystem of banks with varied risk profiles might make the system more resilient, akin to biodiversity in nature. If one species (bank type) falls, it doesn't bring down the whole ecosystem. But fleshing this out requires detailed proposals for how to segment banks by risk appetite, product lines, or liability structures—and how to ensure the state's role doesn't just end up underwriting all these experiments at taxpayers' expense.

6. The "Monoliner" Concept and Systemic Diversity

I want to mention monoliners here —banks specializing narrowly in one type of product or lending. Imagine a financial ecology of monoliners: some focus on short-term commercial paper, others on medium-term mortgages, and others on long-term infrastructure lending. Each would have risk parameters aligned with their product horizons, and they might fund themselves with instruments that match those horizons. The state or central bank's job could then be to ensure that no single shock in one sector cascades uncontrollably.

This vision could reduce systemic risk by avoiding the one-size-fits-all universal banking model. Yet it would require a radical restructuring of banking charters, capital rules, and supervisory practices. If Summers' hint at increased risk tolerance for individual banks is a nudge in this direction, we need more detail: how do we ensure monoliners remain viable, transparent, and not subject to hidden contagion through off-balance-sheet instruments or interbank exposures? Without detail, it remains just a clever concept without a roadmap.

7. Moving Beyond Summaries to Architecture

Summers (and many in similar positions) often present a string of "interesting topics"—maturity transformation, narrow banking, cross-border regulation—without walking us through the actual mechanics of change. Without returning to "first principles" (why certain structures were created, how they were meant to function, and what has changed since), all we get are half-acknowledged dilemmas without solutions.

The real work lies in reimagining the foundational logic of the banking system for a 21st-century context. It demands new frameworks that:

- Encourage diversity in bank business models without losing sight of systemic stability.

- Redefine the roles and responsibilities of the private sector, the state, and the central bank.

- Address globalization and cross-border finance with coherent international standards.

- Consider radical alternatives like narrow banking and test their feasibility in a technologically advanced, highly mobile capital environment.

Until we delve into these details, every mention of these points—no matter how seemingly insightful—risks becoming a footnote in a never-ending status quo, rather than a genuine blueprint for the future.

VIII. Regulatory Challenges and Systemic Fragility

A crucial dynamic: beneath the surface of these policy discussions lies a fundamental misalignment in how U.S. banking and financial regulation evolves (or fails to evolve). Let's break down the layers:

1. The Absence of a Coherent National Strategy

Summers' comment about future growth of international institutions over local ones and the dominance of federal over state banks is superficially stating a trend we've all seen: the U.S. (and the world) has shifted toward larger, more globally connected financial entities. But the U.S. regulatory apparatus hasn't adjusted accordingly—its fragmented structure remains rooted in a bygone era.

- **Federal vs. State-Level Fragmentation:** In the U.S., each state has its own banking regulator, statutes, and political agendas. States, often driven by local electoral cycles, have no incentive to align their strategies with federal goals or global realities. Their prime KPI is not delivering a robust, future-proof financial system—it's about maintaining a short-term, favorable local status quo that appeals to voters and local interest groups.

- **The Resulting Status Quo Bias:** Without a unified national vision—let alone an international one—the system defaults to what's comfortable. The Fed, FDIC, and Treasury act as patchwork managers, intervening sporadically but lacking a long-term blueprint. This vacuum of strategy at the top fosters protectionism and incremental tinkering rather than bold reform.

2. Regulatory Inertia and Political Economy

My observation about regulators who are "just trying to get re-elected" or secure their own positions touches on the political economy of banking regulation.

- **Local Political Incentives Over Systemic Goals:** State regulators, who may be appointed or operate in a politically charged environment, often measure success by local economic metrics or political "wins." If they can show they're "better" than other states—or at least not the worst—that's enough to justify their approach. They rarely ask: "How do we make the U.S. banking sector globally competitive, resilient, and innovation-friendly?" Instead, they angle for incremental improvements that maintain their office and power base.

- **Protectionism and Rent-Seeking:** In this environment, entrenched incumbents (existing banks) have every incentive to lobby for regulations that shield them from competition—be it from neighboring states, foreign banks, fintech upstarts, or crypto players. Politicians and regulators, in turn, benefit from the patronage of these local institutions. The result is a regulatory framework that protects the old guard and shuns meaningful evolution.

3. The Confusing Case of SVB and State-level Action

The SVB scenario showcases these tensions. A state-level regulator pulled SVB's license—understandable on paper, since that's within their jurisdiction. But in practical terms, SVB was massive for that state and its customer base. Instead of a coordinated, planned resolution, the situation quickly escalated to the FDIC stepping in, raising questions about the interplay between state and federal authorities.

Conspiracy or Just Poor Coordination?: It's not necessarily a conspiracy, but the confusion arises because there's no clear, unified protocol for handling the fall of a major bank that straddles state and federal lines. SVB's collapse happened in an era where cross-border deposit flows, digital banking, and interlinked portfolios are common, yet we still rely on outdated regulatory seams. This lack of a cohesive crisis strategy invites speculation, mistrust, and even conspiracy theories. It's the natural outcome when no one has a strong strategic compass.

4. The Reluctance to Engage with Emerging Sectors: Crypto, Stablecoins, CBDC

Summers' point about regulatory hesitance to even discuss certain industries (like crypto) because acknowledging them confers a form of legitimacy.

- **Delaying Tactics and Silent Endorsement:** Just by entertaining a debate around stablecoins or CBDCs, regulators risk validating these innovations. Their chosen tactic—stalling and dismissing—works to preserve the status quo. But by refusing an open, structured conversation, they also forego shaping these emerging fields in a way that could benefit the public interest. They end up ceding the narrative to market forces and foreign regulators who are less timid.

- **From Protecting Society to Protecting Incumbents:** Regulation should ideally protect citizens and the integrity of the financial system. Yet when regulators refuse to engage, it often looks like they're protecting incumbents (traditional banks) from disruption. Instead of setting standards and ensuring new technologies are safe and beneficial, they hide behind silence. This approach can stifle innovation and ultimately harm consumers who might benefit from better, cheaper, or more inclusive financial products.

5. The Need for a Strategic Vision and Architecture

What's missing is a top-down reconsideration: what should the U.S. banking sector be in 10 or 20 years? Who are we serving, and how do we maintain global competitiveness while ensuring stability and fairness?

- **Comparative Advantage and Global Positioning:** Global banking is changing rapidly. Other jurisdictions (the EU, UK, Singapore, Hong Kong, even emerging markets) experiment with regulatory sandboxes, digital asset frameworks, and integrated cross-border regulatory regimes. Without a national strategy, the U.S. risks slipping behind, relying on old logic and local patchwork to navigate a globally competitive landscape.

- **Institutional Memory and First Principles:** We've lost track of why the Federal Reserve was created, why deposit insurance exists, and why banks are structured the way they are. Without revisiting these first principles, every policy tweak is just another piece of duct tape. A serious review might ask: Do we still need 50 sets of state-level banking regulations in a digital, mobile world? How do we foster healthy competition and innovation without exposing society to undue risk?

6. Toward a More Adaptive Regulatory Framework

If the U.S. wants to recapture its dynamism, it must embrace a more adaptive, principles-based regulatory framework. This doesn't mean deregulation. It means clear-eyed regulation that understands technology, globalization, and capital mobility:

- **A Cohesive National (and International) Dialogue:** Encourage federal and state regulators to align incentives toward a common strategic goal. This might involve new federal frameworks that streamline certain aspects of banking oversight, incentivizing states to coordinate rather than compete purely on local interests.

- **Global Cooperation:** Move beyond domestic siloed thinking. Engage in meaningful dialogue with foreign regulators to create more coherent international standards. The conversation isn't just about today's biggest banks—it's about the next wave of financial technology, digital currencies, and cross-border lending.

- **Regulate Emerging Sectors Openly and Proactively:** Instead of avoiding crypto and stablecoins, regulators could set conditional guidelines, pilot programs, or safe zones that allow these innovations to develop responsibly. By shaping the terrain early, regulators gain more control and ensure that consumer protection and systemic resilience are baked in from the start.

My critique exposes the hollow center of current U.S. financial regulation—a world where each regulator, especially at the state level, clings to their narrow status quo, while the federal agencies rarely present a visionary, future-proof roadmap. The result is a system that is reactive, protective of incumbents, and ill-prepared for the rapid changes in the global financial marketplace. Without a rekindling of first principles and a courageous step toward strategic, long-term thinking, the U.S. risks entrenching a dysfunctional status quo. It's precisely this kind of deeper, detail-oriented re-imagination that thought leaders like Summers allude to but never fully deliver.

IX. Systemic Problems and Leadership Inaction

A core cognitive and epistemological challenge—one that affects not only banking leaders, but experts in any domain. It's about how institutions, norms, and systems evolve through historical happenstance, crisis-driven patchwork, and unplanned adaptations, and how, over time, these "accidents" harden into unquestioned truths. Once established, these truths are upheld and defended by experts whose authority partly depends on the stability and credibility of the current narrative, rather than on challenging it.

1. The Myth of Deliberate Design

In retrospect, many elements of the banking infrastructure appear as if they were designed with a grand vision in mind. The existence of certain regulatory frameworks, capital requirements, deposit insurance schemes, and central bank mandates seem to arise from rational planning. But often, they didn't. They resulted from responses to emergencies, opportunistic political deals, and path-dependent historical quirks. Over time, these patchwork solutions become embedded into the system, rarely questioned because they "work well enough" most of the time.

Experts like Summers appear decades later to explain why these frameworks "must" work this way or to offer post-hoc rationalizations. While some explanations have merit and reflect a true understanding of underlying economic principles, others simply enforce the status quo. This is not necessarily malicious—experts often believe in the narrative themselves. They were raised and trained in an intellectual environment that treats the current system as "the way things are done," rather than one of many possible ways.

2. The Danger of Retrospective Rationalization

Retrospective rationalization is when we look at outcomes that have "worked" and assume they were inevitable or optimal. It's a kind of survivorship bias. In banking, people may say: "This regulatory framework is the best we've got because it has prevented another Great Depression." But the absence of one catastrophic event doesn't prove that the architecture is optimal. It only proves it's been good enough so far—or at least not bad enough to fail dramatically, except for the instances where it does (like SVB).

When an event like SVB's collapse reveals systemic weaknesses, it challenges these tidy narratives. Suddenly, we remember that what exists is not necessarily the result of perfect logic or strategic foresight—it might just have "happened" due to historical contingencies. Yet the system's defenders often rush to downplay or patch the flaw without questioning the deeper logic.

3. The Limits of the Expert Mindset

Experts—especially those deeply embedded in a field—tend to focus on incremental improvements within the existing framework. Their authority and expertise is often domain-specific. They understand how to tweak interest rates, adjust capital ratios, and manage liquidity crises within the current paradigm. They are less inclined to question the paradigm itself. Doing so would require stepping outside their comfort zone and risking intellectual and professional capital.

This phenomenon extends beyond banking. Your tennis coach's explanation for the lack of Black players in top tennis in 1990 wasn't the product of overt racism or bad intention; it was just a simplistic interpretation of the status quo. He took the current reality—few Black players at the top—and translated it into a "fact" about why things are the way they are. He didn't consider historical exclusion, socio-economic factors, access to facilities, representation, or systemic biases. Similarly, many banking leaders don't consider how legacy systems and historical compromises shape the current structure. They see the world as it is and assume it's natural.

4. Asking the Bigger "Why?"

To move beyond superficial expert explanations, we need to constantly ask: "Why did this system come to be?" "What constraints, historical accidents, or power dynamics shaped it?" and "Is there another way?" This involves stepping outside narrow disciplinary thinking and incorporating insights from history, sociology, political science, and even anthropology. In the case of banking, it might mean re-examining how the Federal Reserve's role evolved over a century of political pressures, wars, technological changes, and crises. It might mean asking what purpose deposit insurance served originally and whether it still fits the modern financial ecosystem.

Such questioning is uncomfortable for many experts, because it may reveal that a beloved principle or cherished model is not, in fact, an immutable truth but a historically contingent workaround. It demands a willingness to embrace uncertainty, complexity, and the possibility that "the way things are" isn't the only way.

5. The Broader Lesson: Beyond Banking

Let's do some comparison here to discussions about the limits of science and the scientific approach highlights that this isn't just a banking or finance issue. Any domain—scientific disciplines, policy frameworks, cultural norms—can fall into this trap. Science, for instance, progresses by questioning assumptions, running experiments, and allowing new evidence to reshape paradigms. When science becomes dogmatic, it stops being effective. Similarly, when finance experts become complacent, believing their current system is the natural, best-in-class outcome, they stop seeing alternative architectures that might better serve society.

6. The Value of Fresh Perspectives and Interdisciplinary Thinking

Real innovation often comes from outsiders or from insiders who dare to think like outsiders—those who are not fully invested in the status quo. By stepping back and considering first principles, alternative models, or even radical ideas like narrow banking or international regulatory cooperatives, thinkers challenge the status quo. They force us to recognize that so many elements of the current system are not eternal truths but historical artifacts.

The SVB collapse and the ensuing commentary from people like Summers have shone a light on the deeper, systemic nature of the problem. They show how certain institutions are taken for granted because they've "just happened" over time. True understanding—and potentially better solutions—emerge when we question these inheritances. Instead of treating the status quo as a product of deliberate, optimal design, we must see it as the accumulation of compromises, reactions, and accidents. Only then can we start imagining something different, something better.

X. Monoliners and Systemic Risk: A Better Understanding

On something vital that the "Captain Obvious" critiques tend to gloss over: the deeper systemic role of specialization and risk-taking in banking. It's too easy to say "SVB failed because it focused too narrowly on a single industry" or "SVB held too many uninsured deposits." Yes, those statements are true at the surface level, but they don't get to the heart of why specialization (monoliners) and the existence of higher-risk, niche banks can actually contribute to the overall health, resilience, and innovation of the financial system.

1. Specialization vs. Homogenization

A major advantage of "monoliners"—banks that concentrate on a specific industry, technology vertical, or customer niche—is that they become experts in understanding those clients' needs and risks. This depth of knowledge can lead to better-tailored financial products and more informed lending decisions within that niche, contributing to the efficient allocation of capital. Could a large, "universal" bank that dabbles superficially across many sectors provide that same level of insight, relationship-building, or innovation? Probably not. By offering specialized services and flexible, industry-specific solutions, these niche players help new and dynamic segments of the economy flourish.

2. Systemic Resilience Through Diversity

Diversity in an ecosystem isn't just about superficial appearances—it's about resilience. In biology, monocultures are prone to collapse if a single disease strikes. Similarly, a banking system composed entirely of identical, risk-averse, broad-spectrum banks might seem stable, but it's actually more fragile: if one systemic shock hits a universal banking model, it could rattle the entire sector uniformly.

In contrast, a system that includes a variety of monoliners, each experimenting with different types of risk and different customer segments, can actually be more stable at the macro level. If one specialized institution fails, it may fail in isolation without toppling all the others. Because each monoliner is exposed to different types of risk, the correlation of failures should be lower. SVB's downfall, painful though it was, didn't cause a cascade of identical failures. Instead, it raised the question: how do we absorb this shock in a way that strengthens the system, not weakens it?

3. Innovation Through Risk-Taking and Experimentation

Progress requires experiments, and experiments often require someone willing to take on risk. Niche banks that specialize in emerging technologies, underserved markets, or unconventional lending models test hypotheses that the big, risk-averse players wouldn't touch. When such a bank succeeds, it can open a whole new field of opportunity for the broader market, demonstrating that a previously overlooked sector can be profitable and stable with the right approach.

This is similar to innovation in any industry: it's often smaller, more specialized players that pioneer new methods, technologies, and frameworks. If the regulatory environment were to discourage specialized, risk-taking banks, we'd lose an essential force for growth and adaptation in the financial ecosystem. Without these "stalkers" (scouts) who push forward into uncharted territory, the entire system might stagnate.

4. Rethinking the Regulator's Role

This leads us back to the regulator. The choice isn't between laissez-faire indifference and micromanagement, but between a static, reactive posture and a dynamic, forward-looking strategy. Regulators can acknowledge the systemic value of monoliners and design frameworks that let these banks experiment—within defined safety nets. They can provide guidance, backstops, or shared platforms for risk mitigation without stamping out innovation.

- **Risk-Sharing Mechanisms:** Imagine if regulators created targeted liquidity facilities or insurance pools that specialized banks could tap during stress events. The goal would be to prevent isolated failures from becoming systemic panics, while not forcing every bank into the same low-risk, generic mold.

- **Smarter Capital Requirements:** Instead of a one-size-fits-all approach, regulators could tailor capital requirements to reflect the unique risk profiles of specialized banks. This wouldn't eliminate risk, but would encourage responsible risk-taking, ensuring monoliners keep adequate buffers without killing their innovative edge.

5. Beyond the $250k Deposits Limit

Simply pointing out that SVB held too many uninsured deposits is a trivial observation. It's like saying a highly specialized biotech company is fragile because it relies on venture funding. True, but that's also how biotech innovation happens—through risk-tolerant capital. Similarly, if we responded to SVB by insisting every bank only hold fully insured deposits, we'd end up with a legion of identical, ultra-cautious banks that never fund anything genuinely new.

Instead, regulators and policymakers should ask: How can we preserve the value that monoliners bring while mitigating the downsides? How can we create a system in which specialization and risk-taking are safely accommodated? Maybe that means more transparency about banks' risk profiles, more dynamic deposit insurance structures that vary with bank type, or new ways to quickly resolve failed institutions without rattling the entire system.

6. The Big Picture: Stepping Beyond Captain Obvious

The "Captain Obvious" critiques frame SVB's collapse as a simple tale of concentration risk and too many uninsured deposits: the deeper story is about system design. A healthy financial system should resemble an ecosystem with varied species, each playing its role. Some specialize in niches, take bigger risks, and either reap big rewards or fail spectacularly—providing valuable lessons and paths forward. The regulator's job, then, isn't to eliminate such failures outright, but to ensure that when they occur, they don't destabilize the entire system and that the lessons learned spur better regulation and market practices going forward.

In other words, SVB's collapse should not push us toward bland uniformity or a risk-free gray landscape. Instead, it should prompt us to think more creatively about how to enable healthy diversity in banking models, how to encourage (and contain) productive risk-taking, and how to ensure that when one specialized player stumbles, the rest of the system doesn't go down with it. That's the conversation we should be having—far more interesting and productive than just observing the obvious after the fact.

XI. The Fed, Rumors, and Bailout Economics

Several deeper issues about the role of the Federal Reserve, the nature of bank runs (both rational and rumor-driven), and the complex reality behind government interventions like bailouts. Let's try to unravel these layers:

1. The Rumor-Driven Vulnerability and the Fed's Role

Summers states, quite rightly, that **rumors can kill a bank**. Any bank's business model, based on fractional reserves and long-term investments funded by short-term deposits, is inherently vulnerable to a confidence crisis. If depositors believe others are about to withdraw, they rush to do the same—triggering a self-fulfilling prophecy. It's a structural vulnerability of modern banking.

Then where is the Fed in all this? Ideally, the Fed and other regulators exist precisely to prevent self-fulfilling panics that arise from fear rather than fundamentals. In theory, a central bank as the "lender of last resort" can provide emergency liquidity to calm markets. By doing so, it stops rumor-induced runs before they snowball. Yet the SVB case (and others before it) begs the question: if the Fed is slow or cautious to intervene, or if it only acts after the panic is well underway, what's the point?

This is where the metaphor of the "pussy cop" comes in. If the regulator talks tough when confronting petty infractions (like slapping the wrist of a small-time thief) but disappears when the real gangs show up, it undermines the credibility of the entire enforcement system. Similarly, if the Fed is good at imposing rules after the fact, or penalizing minor non-systemic misdeeds, but seems absent or indecisive in the face of a genuine systemic panic, it raises fundamental questions about its purpose. Rumors, by definition, spread quickly—regulators need to be swift and decisive. If they fail to be, the entire premise of having a central backstop comes under scrutiny.

2. The Media-Savvy Client Base: Information Flows and Responsibility

Summers' observation that SVB's client base was "media-savvy" points to a new twist in the old bank-run narrative. Today's depositors aren't just reacting to hushed chatter in a local pub; they're reacting to high-velocity information spreads over Twitter, Slack channels, and private investor groups. Rapid information dissemination can trigger near-instantaneous outflows. Is that the fault of the bank, the customers, or the regulator?

- **Toxicity of the Valley Party?:** The question of Silicon Valley's role is tricky. On one hand, it's a place that thrives on rapid decision-making and constant information sharing, which can accelerate a panic. On the other hand, fast, open communication is part of the DNA of innovation hubs.

- **Responsibility of Mouthpieces:** If a prominent tech figure tweets "Run for the exits," do they bear responsibility for the ensuing panic? Legal responsibility may be limited, but moral responsibility and reputational considerations come into play. In a world where everyone has a platform, how do we encourage responsible communication without stifling free information flow?

3. The Government "Bailouts" That Make Money (Eventually)

I want to highlight a 'fascinating' point often missed in the simplistic "bailout" narrative: Historically, many government interventions—especially in 2008—didn't end up costing taxpayers in the long run. Take the TARP program, for example. The U.S. Treasury bought distressed assets at a time of panic. As the market recovered, these assets were often sold at a profit. In many cases, the interventions ended up netting gains for the government, and by extension, taxpayers.

- **A Market Mechanism, Not Pure Charity:** Instead of viewing these interventions as handouts, it can be more accurate to see them as strategic market participants stepping in at times of extraordinary stress. The government, with its unique ability to hold assets longer and absorb short-term risk, can stabilize markets and eventually profit.

- **Counterintuitive for the Public:** The public perception often diverges from the economic reality. People hear "bailout" and imagine taxpayer money vanishing into a black hole. Politicians and commentators who say "privatized gains and socialized losses" feed a popular narrative of injustice. Sometimes that narrative is warranted, especially when reckless banks or executives walk away rich. But at other times, it's a misleading oversimplification that ignores the fact that these interventions can—and have—yielded net positive returns.

4. "Privatized Gains, Socialized Losses"—Populist Rhetoric or Real Concern?

The phrase "privatized gains and socialized losses" has become a kind of shorthand for moral hazard: if bankers know the government will step in to save them, they'll take more risks. But not every intervention fits this neat mold. The interlocutor's suggestion that calling every intervention a "bailout" or "socialized loss" is simplistic is on point.

- **Moral Hazard vs. Necessary Stabilization:** If the state steps in, buys assets at fire-sale prices, stabilizes markets, and eventually sells those assets at a profit, is that really just socializing the losses? Or is it acting as a counter-cyclical stabilizer that prevents deeper systemic damage and eventually returns money to the public purse?

- **Populism and the Perception Gap:** Populist narratives flourish because financial systems are complex and opaque. The public doesn't easily see the final balance sheets of these interventions; they only recall the headlines of "bailouts" at the time of crisis. Smart players can exploit this gap in understanding to stir resentment or shape political outcomes.

5. The Regulator's Role in Shaping Outcomes and Narratives

Summers (and many similar commentators) points out truths—like rumors can kill a bank or that bailouts can be profitable—but often leaves the deeper systemic discussion unexplored. These points raise questions about the fundamental responsibilities of the Fed, the nature of financial innovation, the role of quick, rumor-driven panics in a hyper-connected era, and the complexity of government interventions. All this brings us back to the regulator—what is the Fed's role, really?

- **Proactive vs. Reactive:** If rumors can kill a bank, the Fed should be more than a silent watcher. It should be prepared to step in as a lender of last resort before a crisis spirals, communicate clearly to calm markets, and work with other regulators to ensure a coordinated response. If it allows a rumor-driven panic to topple an otherwise solvent institution, it's failing in its fundamental purpose.

- **Public Communication and Confidence:** The Fed and other regulators must also communicate clearly to the public why certain interventions aren't just handouts to the reckless. They need to highlight the final outcomes, the profits realized, and the systemic benefits. Without transparency and education, the public discourse will remain dominated by simplistic tropes that may lead to suboptimal policy down the line.

To build a resilient and just financial system, we need to move beyond simplistic narratives. Recognize that sometimes the state intervenes not to coddle banks, but to stabilize a chaotic market and can even profit in the long run. Accept that monoliners and specialized institutions bring systemic innovation and diversity. And hold the Fed and other regulators accountable for preventing rumor-driven collapses. Only then can we elevate the conversation beyond cheap populism and superficial truisms.

XII. Embracing the Reality of Our Fictions

A tension that lies at the very foundation of modern financial systems: the delicate balance between truth, trust, and the psychological scaffolding that keeps society functioning. Let's break it down:

1. The Illusion of Full Insurance

The idea of fully insuring all deposits is seductive—no depositor panic, no runs on the bank, just a perfect safety net. But as you may point out, insurance itself is always a bet against uncertainty. Any insurer, whether the FDIC or a private firm, operates on probabilities and reserves. If everyone demands their insured claims simultaneously, the structure collapses. At scale, it's never a question of actual full coverage; it's about making people believe the coverage is there and will be honored under "normal" stress scenarios. In extreme systemic crises, the insurer (FDIC included) cannot unilaterally cover all losses. The entire premise of insurance—financial or otherwise—relies on not everyone hitting the panic button at the same time.

2. The Role of Psychological Comfort

The guarantee, the presence of experts, and even the authoritative complexity of someone like Summers talking shop, serve a psychological function. They provide reassurance, a narrative that things are "under control," that someone knowledgeable is at the helm, and that the system (however opaque or precarious) is at least not immediately collapsing. Human societies have always had such mechanisms: religious rites, social contracts, expert testimony. They're not solely about objective truth; they're about emotional and psychological stability.

From that perspective, deposit insurance isn't just a financial instrument. It's a psychological trick that helps maintain the day-to-day functioning of the economy. Without it, given how fractional banking works, people might perpetually teeter on the edge of paranoia, hoarding cash under mattresses or refusing to engage in the financial system at all.

3. The "Adult" vs. "Childish" Position

Are people ready to face the raw truth of systemic fragility? Or do they prefer a comforting narrative that encourages them to continue participating—opening accounts, investing, consuming—without collapse into dread or nihilism?

Most people choose the latter, perhaps implicitly. Whether consciously or not, consumers prefer not to have the full sobering truth rubbed in their faces. They know the world is complicated, that not every deposit is 100% safe if everything falls apart. Yet they rely on social institutions to maintain a façade of order and reassurance. This is not necessarily bad. It's a practical compromise. Societies function because people accept a baseline narrative of stability that lets them make everyday decisions without existential dread.

4. The Cost of Truth

What would happen if we told every depositor the unvarnished truth at account opening?

- They'd learn that deposit insurance is limited and could fail under extreme duress.

- They'd learn that currencies, themselves, rely on confidence and are subject to inflation, devaluation, or even collapse under certain conditions.

- They'd learn about systemic leverage and the complexity that no single regulator or expert fully controls.

Knowing all this could lead to paralysis, panic, or withdrawal from the financial system. Widespread fear would be economically catastrophic. The delicate dance is to provide enough transparency to maintain trust, but not so much brutal honesty that it triggers self-defeating panic.

5. The Humanist Perspective

From a humanist standpoint, the existence of these "heretical" fictions—insurance that can't pay everyone at once, experts who maintain confidence even if their words are partly theater—is a necessity. Societies run on trust and narrative as much as on rational calculation. If people truly confronted the full fragility and contingency of all social constructs, they might give up on cooperation, investment, and long-term planning—activities that are essential to a functioning civilization.

Paradoxically, this means that "lies" or "half-truths" can have social value. They aren't always malicious deceptions; sometimes they're stabilizing myths. The trick is not to become cynical about it, but to acknowledge that part of the social contract involves accepting workable illusions that help us all get on with our lives.

The banking system, deposit insurance, and expert pronouncements are not solely about ironclad guarantees and empirical truths. They are instruments for maintaining equilibrium in a world where total security cannot exist. People often don't want the full truth—nor could they handle it en masse without ripping apart the delicate fabric of economic life.

We can criticize this arrangement, try to improve transparency, and reduce unnecessary complexity. But at some fundamental level, we must recognize that human societies need these psychological underpinnings. They need a sense of safety, even if it's partly constructed, to keep functioning. A purely "adult" approach—full truth, full accountability, no comforting illusions—would be socially destabilizing. Thus, we accept a compromise: knowing deep down that these assurances are partial truths, yet embracing them so that tomorrow the shops open, the jobs continue, and life goes on.

XIII. The Question of Small and Medium-sized Banks vs. Mega-banks (or Monoliners vs. Specialized?)

A vision for a structural rethinking of banking that separates the functions of payment infrastructure (the "mint" role) and the creation of specialized financial products and services (the "bank" role). Let's break down the concepts and the trade-offs involved.

1. The Idea of Direct Fed Accounts (Payment Infrastructure)

The podcast (with Summers) suggests separating checking (transactional) accounts from savings (deposit, investment) accounts. One extreme version of this is having everyone's checking account directly at the Federal Reserve—a "FedAccount" system. The private banks would then handle lending, savings products, and other services, but not basic payments and custody of funds.

- **Clarity of Roles:**

Currently, the line between "pure payment infrastructure" and "banking products" is blurred. Banks provide both the ledger of your money (checking accounts) and manage risk-taking activities (lending, maturity transformation). Splitting these roles could increase transparency and reduce confusion for customers who often don't understand that their checking account money is being lent out long-term by the bank.

- **Resilience and Stability:**

If the Fed provides the ledger for checking accounts, depositors are essentially holding cash at the central bank. In theory, no bank run can threaten these transactional balances, because they are not on a private bank's balance sheet. If a private bank fails, customers can be reassigned to another service provider without losing access to their transactional funds.

- **Regulatory Simplicity and Data Integrity:**

A direct fed ledger would allow regulators real-time oversight of aggregate money balances, reducing the reporting lag and complexity. No more relying solely on "trust" and after-the-fact reporting from banks.

Downsides and Concerns (vs Rationale for This Separation):

- **Innovation and Service Quality:**

A central bank is not designed to offer innovative financial services, products, or personalized experiences to customers. Historically, public sector entities are not as nimble or customer-focused as private-sector competitors. If the Fed ran everyone's transaction accounts directly, you risk a stagnant environment with little incentive for innovation.

- **Competition and Monopolization of Payments:**

The Fed controlling the fundamental payment layer could stifle private competition in that realm. While efficiency might improve, you lose the dynamic, evolutionary processes that occur when multiple players compete on user experience, integration, and auxiliary services.

2. Monoliners and Specialized Banking Services

Instead of universal banks doing everything—lending across all sectors, payment services, investment advisory, etc.—you're proposing a system of monoline banks. Each specialized institution would focus on a certain type of lending or customer niche, presumably delivering superior knowledge, service, and product design.

- **Expertise and Customer Fit:**

A specialized lender that deeply understands a particular industry, region, or product can create more value and better risk models than a one-size-fits-all universal bank.

- **Systemic Diversification:**

A financial ecosystem with many monoliners reduces correlated risks. If one monoliner focused on, say, renewable energy startups fails due to a sector-specific downturn, it doesn't necessarily topple banks focused on agriculture or real estate.

- **Encouraging Innovation:**

Monoline institutions, focused on their niche, might be more willing to experiment, find new markets, and adapt quickly—driving overall financial system innovation.

Risks and Challenges (vs Benefits) of Monoliners:

- **Higher Individual Risk:**

A monoliner's concentration in one sector or product line makes it more vulnerable to sector-specific downturns. This higher volatility is expected and can be mitigated by the broader system's diversity, but individual customers must understand these risks.

- **Consumer Clarity and Education:**

Customers would need to become more aware of differences between institutions. With more specialized players, how do consumers navigate a banking landscape that's not based on "one big bank does it all" but "a hundred small specialists each do one thing really well"?

3. The Question of Small and Medium-Sized Banks vs. Mega-Banks

Do we need a large number of small and medium-sized banks, or should we consolidate into a few big institutions (like Canada's model)?

- **The Traditional U.S. Model:**

Historically, the U.S. banking landscape is extremely fragmented due to past regulations that limited interstate banking. This created many community and regional banks that served local needs. While this had benefits for localism and credit availability, today's digitized economy might not need so many regionally bound institutions.

- **Consolidation and Efficiency:**

Fewer, larger institutions can achieve economies of scale, uniform standards, and simpler regulatory oversight. Some argue this leads to greater stability and easier governance, as in Canada's heavily regulated oligopoly of large banks.

- **Diversity and Innovation Argument:**

A counter-argument is that a homogenous landscape of a few giant banks reduces system resilience and innovation. "Too big to fail" emerges, and competition suffers. Many small and medium monoliners could provide a more vibrant ecosystem, adapting to niche opportunities and spreading out systemic risk.

4. Finding a Balance

The proposal to separate checking accounts (as stable, ledger-only functions) and savings/lending functions (as innovative, specialized, risk-taking enterprises) aims to clarify risk distribution and upgrade the financial infrastructure.

- **A Centralized Payment Ledger (FedAccount) with Distributed Product Innovation:**

The ideal might be: the Fed acts as a basic ledger keeper (like a public utility), ensuring transactional money safety and transparency. On top of this stable foundation, a wide variety of specialized private banks compete to offer savings products, loans, credit lines, investment tools, and more. They can innovate and specialize without threatening the basic payment infrastructure.

- **International Comparisons and Telecom Analogy:**

Similar to telecommunications where phone numbers became portable and the "core identity" (the number) moved with you, a central ledger of accounts at the Fed would ensure that customer identity and transactional ability is a stable baseline. Banks become like MVNOs—competing to offer better services on top of the stable infrastructure. However, unlike giving everything to the Ministry of Communications (which kills private innovation), you maintain a marketplace of private financial service providers who leverage the stable core.

In short, my vision: a stable central ledger controlled by the Fed for basic transaction accounts, combined with a thriving ecosystem of specialized, monoline financial institutions offering diverse and innovative products, could strike a balance between security, innovation, and choice. This stands in contrast to both the current fragmentation of U.S. banking and the heavily consolidated Canadian model.

- Having more specialized monoline banks, rather than a few large universal or regional institutions, could spur innovation, provide better customer fits, and enhance systemic resilience through diversity.

- However, one must balance innovation with oversight, ensure that consumers are educated enough to choose wisely, and maintain a role for the Fed (or central regulator) as the stable cornerstone of the monetary system.

XIV. The Fed's Role in Systemic Stability

Circling back to a central theme: the SVB collapse acts as a magnifying lens, not just on one bank's management or one "industry" ecosystem, but on the entire regulatory and systemic framework that's supposed to ensure stability. In a sense, SVB becomes a litmus test for the Federal Reserve (and other regulators): what do they stand for, what's their plan, and why have them if they can't prevent a panic that's well within the realm of foreseeable events?

1. Political Clout and Status Quo Preservation

Small and regional banks wield disproportionate political influence in the U.S.: the Senate's alignment with local banking interests results in regulatory inertia. This explains why, instead of stepping back and rethinking fundamentals, policymakers often default to defending the status quo. These smaller institutions don't necessarily have strategic long-term visions; their lobbying is about maintaining what currently exists, even if it no longer serves the economy's evolving needs. The political system's resistance to change stems as much from these entrenched interests as it does from any lack of economic insight.

2. Revolutionaries Running Back to the Old System

"Innovators" who talk a big game about building a parallel financial system still run to the Fed and the FDIC when trouble hits is spot-on: it exposes the gap between rhetoric and reality. The "new financial order," whether it's in crypto or alternative banking, often rests on assumptions that they can circumvent legacy systems. But when panic hits, trust and liquidity still gravitate toward the central backstop—the Fed and the FDIC. This paradox reveals that these so-called revolutionaries haven't truly transcended the old model. They've built atop it, and when their scaffolding cracks, they cling to the old support beams.

3. SVB's "Failure" as a Mirror of the System

SVB's biggest sin was lacking a forward-looking strategy and essentially drifting along with market growth. But as you can note, that's hardly unique—and not grounds for immediate destruction. If we shot every actor who lacked purpose, the entire system, including the Fed, would be empty. The Fed itself has shown little in the way of a coherent long-term vision—it reacts, fire-fighting style, crisis after crisis.

Moreover, SVB's collapse came from a "technical gap," a temporary mismatch that should have been addressable within the established rules. Full-reserve banking is not the norm; composite balances are. If the game is set up this way, occasional liquidity mismatches are not a deviation—they're part of the model. Banks rely on central banks to smooth these bumps. If the regulator stands by and watches a run triggered by rumor, or fails to provide timely liquidity support for a solvable mismatch, it begs the question: why have a regulator at all?

4. Rumors, Runs, and the Fed's Absence

The two universal truths in banking collapses are:

- Liquidity can be drained quickly if panic sets in.
- Rumors can ignite that panic.

A credible central backstop (the Fed) is supposed to preempt or quell these fires. That's the entire historical rationale for a central bank: lender of last resort, provider of confidence, the stabilizer of last resort. If the Fed doesn't step in promptly when a healthy but temporarily illiquid institution is under attack—what's the point? If a big part of systemic stability depends on perception and psychology, the central bank must be quick and decisive in its interventions. Procrastination or indecision makes it complicit in the failure.

5. SVB as a "Model Student" and the School's Failure

SVB was, in many ways, a model of the contemporary banking environment: tech-focused, playing by the accepted rules, holding a standard portfolio of long-duration assets versus short-term deposits. Its sudden downfall due to a technical liquidity gap and rumor-driven run casts doubt not on just SVB's choices, but on the entire structure. If the "model student" flunks out, shouldn't we question the curriculum, the school's policies, and the teaching staff?

Instead of introspection, the Fed and other regulators attempted to externalize the failure. They blame the environment, the uniqueness of SVB's clientele, or the speed of digital withdrawals. But these are known factors—nothing fundamentally new. The inability to adapt or provide timely support is the real failing. By not acting as the backstop they're meant to be, regulators let a preventable collapse escalate into a systemic confidence issue.

6. What's the Fed's Role and Plan?

This brings us full circle: if the Fed exists to maintain stability, ensure liquidity, and prevent rumor-driven failures from becoming systemic crises, where was it when SVB began to falter? If the entire system wobbles when the 16th-largest bank goes under, that indicates a deeper problem. The Fed can either:

- Acknowledge the structural issues and think long-term, revisiting the architecture of banking regulation, the balance of liquidity and maturity transformation, and the transparency of risk.

- Or continue with the status quo, blaming one-off factors, and providing reassurance without real strategy.

My point is that we're seeing a **fundamental failure of imagination** and accountability. The Fed and the broader regulatory apparatus prefer to preserve the current system rather than innovate or accept responsibility for systemic design flaws. With no agenda, no long-term vision, and no willingness to intervene decisively when it matters, they reveal themselves as custodians of inertia, not guardians of stability.

The SVB collapse is less about one bank's poor management and more about what it reveals about the system's stewards. The Fed's non-response (or delayed response) in the face of predictable vulnerabilities and rumor-driven panic suggests a deeper crisis of purpose. If the central bank can't do what it was created to do—prevent runs and maintain confidence—then its strategy, agenda, and even its raison d'être come into question. The SVB episode calls not just for technical fixes, but for a strategic reevaluation of the Fed's role in guiding and stabilizing the financial system long-term. Without that reevaluation, we're left asking: what's the point of having them at all?

XV. Financial System Reform and Central Bank Analysis

A wide-ranging and nuanced critique here of the current financial and monetary architecture, touching on stablecoins, CBDCs, and the structural idiosyncrasies of the U.S. Federal Reserve and its ecosystem of regional banks, Treasury bonds, and payment networks.

1. Stablecoins as a Transitional Proof-of-Concept to CBDCs and Cross-Border Monetary Infrastructure

Let's distill and organize your observations and the implications:

- **Useful but Underdone:** Stablecoins have demonstrated that consumers can separate the *form* of money (the user-facing token) from its *underlying asset* (fiat or other collateral). This conceptual shift paves the way for more radical changes in how we think about and use money.

- **Current Limitations:** So far, stablecoins have been too closely tethered 1:1 to a single currency (like the dollar), preventing the mental leap to a more flexible, composite unit of account. If stablecoins moved toward a basket of currencies (like a "rubric" composed of USD, EUR, JPY, etc.), consumers might better grasp the independence of "form" from "content," aiding a future evolution of monetary frameworks.

- **No True Revolution Yet:** Real, lasting transformation comes through incremental evolution rather than sudden revolution. Stablecoins haven't upended the system—yet. But their existence shows that incremental substitution of one form of money for another is possible, potentially accelerating a future shift to more sophisticated forms of digital money.

- **China's CBDC Strategy:** China's approach to CBDCs suggests central banks might soon lend liquidity directly to foreign institutions—banks, fintechs—expanding their influence beyond their borders. By doing so, a central bank essentially exports its monetary infrastructure, making others dependent on it.

- **From Dollar Hegemony to Infrastructure Hegemony:** Instead of the dollar's role as global common denominator, we could see a world where the infrastructure itself—platforms for issuing, settling, and managing liquidity—becomes the "currency." Countries offering the most compelling infrastructure control the "plumbing" of international finance.

- **Ecosystem as Currency:** In this framework, bonds, infrastructure, and payment rails themselves start to function like currency. Liquidity and trust migrate to robust systems, not just strong economies.

2. The Confusing Hybrid of the U.S. Monetary System: Regulatory Complexity and Fragmentation

Let's start from the Fed and Treasury Misalignment: Treasury issues bonds (term debt with yields) → acts like a borrower. Fed issues currency (effectively perpetual zero-yield liabilities) → acts like a perpetual depositor. This dual structure blends short-term and long-term claims, making the distinction between "money" and "debt" blurry, and reducing overall transparency and accountability.

- **Fed's Nature and Historical Role:** The Federal Reserve is not a monolithic, forward-looking institution; it's a collegial body of 12 regional Feds with historical compromises baked in. Its structure and mandate are inherently reactionary: it must accommodate diverse interests and often looks backward at data and consensus rather than leading with foresight.

- **From an Inter-Bank Utility to a Policy Dictator:**

The Fed started as an inter-bank platform (to coordinate liquidity, prevent bank runs). Over time, it transformed into a powerful central authority. Yet this authority is shaped by outdated structures and interests—federal and state charters, multiple regulators, and legacy payment systems.

- **50+2 State Regulators plus Federal Layers:**

A patchwork of state-level banking regulators, plus the Fed, plus FDIC, plus other agencies, creates a complex web. This leads to inefficiencies, regulatory arbitrage, and difficulty adapting to new technologies or system-wide risks.

- **Licensing, Payment Systems, and Deposit Insurance Not Unified:**

In the U.S., becoming a bank, connecting to a payment network (ACH, FedWire), and obtaining deposit insurance are separate processes involving different authorities and criteria. This contrasts with other countries where a banking license typically covers these essentials.

- **Limited Direct Regulation from the Fed on Charters:**

The Fed influences banks mainly through access to its services (like the Fed master account), not by granting licenses directly. Access to the Fed's balance sheet or discount window becomes a gatekeeper role, giving the Fed indirect, but potent, leverage.

3. Roadblocks to Modernizing Infrastructure

My critique and proposals highlight the need for a fundamental reconsideration of how money, regulation, and infrastructure interact. Instead of persistent confusion and patchwork solutions, you advocate for a transparent, flexible, and modern financial architecture—one that learns from stablecoins and CBDCs, aligns the Fed's structure and mission with contemporary challenges, and streamlines the U.S. regulatory landscape for a future-facing financial system.

- **ACH and FedNow:**

The Fed's attempts to modernize payment rails (e.g., FedNow) face delays due to entrenched interests. Regional banks and founders of legacy systems have an incentive to preserve the status quo.

- **Stagnation vs. Innovation:**

Without a unified vision and simplified structure, the U.S. system struggles to adopt more efficient, resilient payment infrastructures. Innovation is hampered by the fragmentation of authority and the entrenched power of old-school players.

- **Rethink the Core Infrastructure:** Consider an evolved monetary architecture where a central ledger (maintained by a central authority or a consortium) allows frictionless liquidity management and more direct alignment of currency units with their underlying collateral and governance. Move beyond 1:1 stablecoins to multi-currency composites, nudging user perceptions and paving the way for newer forms of money that aren't tied so rigidly to the legacy concept of "the dollar."

- **Refine the Fed's Role:** Move away from the Fed's archaic structure and reactive posture. Clarify the Fed's relationship with the Treasury, possibly separating the functions of issuing short-term and long-term liabilities more transparently. Consider a leaner regulatory environment that can adapt faster, reduce systemic opacity, and integrate new technologies more readily.

- **Infrastructure as the "New Currency":**

Shift the global monetary conversation from one dominated by a single sovereign currency (the dollar) to one where cross-border financial infrastructure, backed by central banks and possibly involving CBDCs, becomes the primary vehicle of trust, efficiency, and dependency.

XVI. The US Banking Sector's Historically Dependent Role

The bewildering patchwork of U.S. financial regulation, where multiple agencies jostle for power, influence, and mandate—often overlapping, sometimes contradicting each other. The result is a fractured system that's the product of historical compromise, political jockeying, and institutional inertia rather than strategic design.

1. FDIC: From Insurer to De-Facto Regulator

Originally, the FDIC was conceived as an insurance entity—protecting depositors and maintaining confidence in the banking system. Over time, it has gained supervisory and quasi-regulatory functions. Its power to grant (and withdraw) deposit insurance essentially gives it leverage to impose conditions on banks. While the FDIC insists it's not a primary regulator, the truth is more ambiguous:

- **Sequential Licensing and Accreditation:**

Unlike other countries where a bank license and deposit insurance approval often happen in parallel, the U.S. system separates these steps. A bank might first get a state charter and then, after proving itself for some years, seek FDIC deposit insurance. That staggered approach effectively puts the FDIC in a gatekeeping role—no insurance, no viable banking model.

- **Choosing Your Primary Regulator:**

The fact that a bank can "opt" which regulator (Fed, FDIC, OCC) takes the lead in supervision is perplexing. This menu of regulators creates a form of regulatory arbitrage: banks can pick the regulator they perceive as most accommodating. By providing insurance, the FDIC secures a foothold to impose conditions, effectively regulating from the back door.

2. FinCEN: The Stealth Enforcer

FinCEN (Financial Crimes Enforcement Network), nominally under the Treasury, wields enormous power via compliance and AML (anti-money laundering) frameworks. Though it doesn't grant licenses or insurance, it can shut down a bank by cutting off access to the financial system if it deems the bank's AML/KYC practices insufficient. It's a "nuclear option" regulator—no official chartering power, but the ability to impose crippling sanctions. This sets up a weird dynamic:

- **De Facto Regulatory Clout:**

    If FinCEN disapproves of a bank's compliance track record, that bank is as good as done. This gives FinCEN enormous, if indirect, regulatory influence, despite it not being framed as a primary banking regulator.

3. OCC: The Would-Be Modernizer Stymied by Lobbyists

The Office of the Comptroller of the Currency (OCC) historically supervised national banks and had a foreign trade focus. In recent years, OCC tried to modernize by introducing new charter types, such as a fintech charter, inspired by frameworks in other jurisdictions like the UK.

- **Blocked by Politics and Lobbies:**

The regional banking lobby and other entrenched interests resisted these changes. The OCC, despite some of the broadest theoretical mandates (it can issue national charters), finds itself bogged down by political blowback whenever it tries to expand or modernize its role.

- **A Natural Regulator for Complex Banking Groups?:**

I suggest the OCC might be more suited to handle "banking groups" or cross-border entities, given its historical perspective. But the OCC's attempts to redefine its role have repeatedly run into obstacles. This is a reflection not just on the OCC's internal capabilities, but also on the complex interplay of American political and economic interests that keep the regulatory mosaic unchanged.

4. A Confused, Layered Regulatory Ecosystem: Why Is It So Messed Up?

This system is not the product of a single coherent vision: it's an accumulated result of over a century of ad hoc legislation, crisis responses, political compromises, and lobbying by entrenched interests (small banks, big banks, states, federal agencies). We end up with a system where:

- State regulators grant charters.

- The Fed looms as a liquidity provider and a "backstop" but often defers frontline regulation to others.

- The FDIC, nominally just an insurer, exercises real power by controlling deposit insurance.

- The OCC can grant national charters but is politically hamstrung.

- FinCEN, technically a unit under the Treasury (which itself issues bonds), can close your bank by cutting off AML compliance lines.

- The SEC, though not in direct competition with banking regulators, governs capital markets and sets another standard for how an effective regulator might look—though with its own issues.

The U.S. banking sector has never been "independent" in the sense of forging its own competitive edge. It thrived because the U.S. economy thrived, not necessarily because the banks were globally best-in-class as stand-alone institutions. They relied on the underlying economic strength, stable currency, and global reserve currency status more than on superior regulatory frameworks or customer focus.

This stands in contrast to the U.S. stock markets, which have had to compete internationally for capital and listings, shaping the SEC into a more singular (though not perfect) entity that defines clearer standards. The SEC's role as a more straightforward, singular securities regulator stands in stark contrast to the overlapping banking regulators, highlighting the complexity in the banking domain as more historical baggage than strategic design.

- The FDIC's morphing into a quasi-regulator underscores the problem of incremental mission creep when agencies are given multiple, sometimes conflicting, mandates.

- FinCEN's powerful but indirect authority shows how "informal" regulatory roles can become decisive.

- The OCC's thwarted attempts at modernization reveal how lobbying and politics keep the regulatory system siloed and resistant to change.

- The U.S. banking sector's reliance on underlying economic strength rather than competitive regulation or innovation means there's little impetus from within the industry to demand a leaner, more coherent regulatory structure.

In conclusion, the U.S. banking regulatory ecosystem is a tangle of legacy institutions, overlapping mandates, and political inertias. Each actor—FDIC, FinCEN, OCC, Fed, and state regulators—carved out their piece of the pie historically and guards it fiercely. Efforts to streamline, modernize, or clarify roles often run into powerful lobbies, political constraints, and the inertia of status quo. This complexity makes episodes like SVB's collapse not just a bank's failure, but a reflection of systemic fragmentation and a call (often unanswered) for a more rationalized approach.

XVII. Separation of State as Owner, Regulator, and Client

I'm outlining here a radical restructuring of the central banking system, one that breaks down the central bank's roles into simpler, more transparent, and more accountable functions.

1. Disaggregating the Central Bank's Roles

Let's walk through the key ideas and implications:

- **Mint / Payment System Function:**

This function focuses purely on issuing the currency and ensuring that the payment infrastructure (from digital ledgers to settlement systems) is stable, transparent, and accessible. Think of it like a public utility: it creates the "circulatory system" of the economy, ensuring money can move easily and reliably. **Key Goal:** Ensure everyone has access to basic monetary services, maintain the integrity of the currency, and guarantee that the infrastructure remains secure and efficient.

- **Central Bank as a Bank (Liquidity Arbitrator):**

The central bank as a "bank of banks" operates a market for liquidity. When some banks have surplus liquidity (excess reserves), the central bank buys it at a certain price; when others have shortfalls, the central bank sells liquidity at a markup. **Key Goal:** Even out short-term liquidity imbalances, preventing unnecessary volatility. **"Burning" Excess Liquidity:** If there's too much liquidity flooding the system, the central bank can "mop it up" by borrowing from banks (paying them interest to hold excess reserves) or by selling them assets at a loss if it wants to absorb more liquidity permanently. This is essentially a monetary policy tool.

- **Ministry of Finance as Regulator and Planner:**

Instead of the central bank being entangled in various conflicting roles, the Ministry of Finance (or Treasury) becomes the main regulatory and strategic planning center. It sets the policy direction and outlines the frameworks and goals but does not directly run the central bank as a profit-seeking enterprise. **Not CFO, More Like COO:** Instead of just "counting the money," the Ministry of Finance would focus on coordinating the broader economic plan—ensuring that the financial system as a whole serves economic development, infrastructure investment, social stability, etc.

State as Company (Borrower) vs. State as Owner (Shareholder): One of the critical reforms I suggest is to cleanly separate the role of the government as a borrower from its role as the "shareholder" or steward of the central banking system.

- **When State Borrows:** The government comes to the market like any other borrower. The central bank can lend surplus liquidity to the government, knowing that there's a risk of default or repayment, just as with any large entity. This prevents automatic monetization of the deficit.

- **When State Manages:** As the ultimate owner, the government (through the Ministry of Finance) sets the long-term economic goals. The central bank's liquidity operations and the "mint" function serve these goals, but do not get mixed up in direct lending to the government as a hidden subsidy.

This clean separation increases transparency. Everyone can see when the government is borrowing for public projects and what the real costs are, rather than blurring it into central bank operations.

2. Encouraging More, Smaller Banks: Surplus or Shortage of Money

By having many smaller banks, you diffuse concentration risk. These smaller institutions can pump smaller amounts of money into various niches of the economy. This fosters competition, innovation, and responsiveness to local credit needs.

- **Benefit:** More granular allocation of capital. If one bank fails or misallocates capital, it doesn't bring down the entire system.

- **Cost/Consideration:** The regulator (Ministry of Finance) and the central bank (liquidity arbitrator) need to ensure robust oversight and risk management frameworks to handle the complexity of a large number of small players.

- **Managing Liquidity at the Macro Level:**

If there's too much money swirling around (inflationary pressure), the central bank's liquidity desk can absorb it by borrowing from banks (offering interest on excess reserves), or by conducting open market operations that permanently retire some liquidity from circulation.

If there's too little money in circulation (deflationary pressure), the central bank can inject liquidity.

Essentially, you're using clear and transparent market operations to keep the "energy" level of the economy balanced.

3. Focus on Real Outcomes, Not Just Profitability: Evolution, Not Revolution

I propose clarifying and simplifying the core roles of the central bank and the government's involvement in finance. By making the central bank functions more explicit (a mint/payment infrastructure utility and a liquidity arbitrator) and separating out the government's role as regulator and borrower, you aim to create a more transparent, stable, and accountable system. This would, in theory, lead to a financial ecosystem better aligned with societal welfare, not obscured by conflicting interests and hidden subsidies.

- **Quality of Life as a Metric:**

Ultimately, you suggest judging the performance of this restructured system by real-world outcomes: Are people engaged, productive, feeling that they are better off today than yesterday?

The central bank in this model is not about turning a profit or accumulating wealth—it's about maintaining the fluid circulation of money that helps everyone get on with their economic lives. Profitability for the central bank is a secondary or even irrelevant metric. Instead, the system's success is measured by economic stability, growth in productive capacities, and an improved standard of living.

- **Practical Considerations:**

Implementing such a restructuring would require careful, incremental changes. Breaking the central bank into separate roles (mint, liquidity bank, etc.) and clarifying the

Ministry of Finance's responsibilities would need new laws, institutional reforms, and public education.

- **Potential Resistance:** The old guard—banks, lobbyists, and certain political factions—might resist losing complexity and opacity because complexity can be profitable and protect incumbents.

It's a vision of finance as a well-structured public utility, infrastructure for commerce, and a caretaker of economic health—rather than a maze of opaque mandates. The ultimate benchmark is real human and economic improvement, not just the comfort of maintaining the status quo.

XVIII. Reforming Central Bank Structure and Strategy

Here is a bold, radical restructuring plan for the U.S. financial system, centered around making the Federal Reserve more transparent, proactive, and strategically driven. My ideas here range from technical fixes (a unified ledger system) to deep institutional reforms (redefining regulatory roles, clarifying responsibilities, and fostering competition).

1. A Unified, Modern Infrastructure for Banking Ledgers

Let's break my proposals down into key pillars and the rationale behind them:

- **One Core-Banking System:**

All banks would operate on a single, standardized ledger platform (or at least fully interoperable ledgers). For smaller or less tech-savvy banks, this provides a free upgrade from archaic systems. For larger, advanced banks, APIs would allow mirroring and backward integration—no loss in functionality.

- **Real-Time Oversight and Reduced Fraud:**

The Fed (or "Fede") would have online, 24/7 access to real-time banking data, eliminating the need for manual, after-the-fact reporting. This reduces opportunities to lie or conceal problems and allows the Fed to detect anomalies early.

- **Instant Transfers and Greater Transparency:**

Unified infrastructure means instant, free, universal transfers for customers—leveling the playing field with countries that already have real-time payments. The Fed could spot liquidity gaps instantly and reassign accounts quickly if a bank fails.

2. Clear and Transparent Regulatory Rules: A More Agile Regulatory Philosophy

- **Rewriting Core Definitions and Rules:**

Clearly define what checking and savings accounts are, what reserves are required, and how banks can manage their balance sheets. Addressing questions like composite balances (mixing different maturity assets and liabilities) must be done upfront. If composite balances are allowed, then the regulator must stand ready to support technical liquidity gaps—no excuses.

- **Regulation Built Into the System:**

By encoding rules directly into the core banking technology (through dashboards and automated compliance checks), regulators and even consumers can monitor key metrics (deposits, loans, capital adequacy) in real-time. Problems can be caught "before the patient dies."

- **Regulator Roles Must Be Clear:**

Decide whether the Fed is just an observer or actually responsible for preventing rumor-driven bank collapses and liquidity shortfalls. If it's the latter, the Fed should be prepared to inject liquidity promptly or combat malicious attacks. If it's the former, that must be openly stated so the market can price that risk.

3. Redefining the Fed's Functions and Strategy, Reforming the Fragmented U.S. Regulatory Landscape

Split the Fed's Functions: Separate the Fed into distinct units:

- **Infrastructure Utility (The "Mint"):** Maintains the ledger, the currency issuance, and the payment rails.

- **Regulatory/Policy Unit:** Sets and enforces rules about bank behavior, liquidity requirements, etc.

- **Liquidity Bank:** Acts as the "market maker" for liquidity, buying low and selling high to stabilize the system, with clear profit/loss accountability or a clear strategic mandate from the state.

- **Articulate a Long-Term Strategy:**

The Fed must determine its growth drivers for the next decade. Is it competing with other central banks for global influence and currency usage? Is it fostering more inclusive finance domestically? Is it scaling the infrastructure to allow foreign banks direct access, thus solidifying the dollar's role through infrastructure rather than just through economic might?

- **Consolidate or Override State Regulators:**

Acknowledge that state-level regulators and overlapping agencies (FDIC, OCC, etc.) are causing friction and backwardness. Either strip them of powers or create a parallel federal track for new entrants—allowing new, monoline banks to get licensed quickly at a federal level and outcompete or absorb outdated regional institutions.

- **Issue Licenses En Masse, Encourage Innovation:**

Following the UK model, granting licenses to numerous new, specialized banks can inject dynamism. Let market forces (guided by transparent rules) weed out the weak and reward the strong. The regulator learns in real-time from market experimentation, rather than stifling it.

- **Adopt a Singapore-Style "Learning by Doing" Approach:**

Anything not explicitly prohibited is allowed, with mandatory notification to the regulator. This ensures the regulator stays informed about market innovations without blocking them upfront. Temporary licenses allow new ideas to flourish while the regulator and market learn together. Later, rules can be refined based on actual outcomes.

- **Adult vs. Child Consumer Treatment:**

Decide how to treat consumers: fully informing them about all risks but expecting them to assume responsibility (adult) or shielding them with deposit insurance and simplified narratives (child). Clarity here shapes the risk culture and consumer expectations.

4. Integrate Dollar and Bond Transparency: Compete Globally by Offering Infrastructure

My proposals outline a future where the Fed and U.S. regulatory environment evolve from a tangled, backward-looking patchwork into a streamlined, transparent, technology-driven ecosystem. By unifying the core banking infrastructure, rewriting and embedding rules directly into the system, clarifying institutional roles, and embracing innovation (both domestically and internationally), you aim to create a robust, agile, and strategically guided financial system.

- **Make the Dollar and Treasuries More Transparent:**

The dollar, heavily influenced by U.S. bond markets, could be reconceived as a form of "transcript" or "receipt" linked to the country's economic performance and balance sheet. Provide clear reporting: revenues, expenses, debt-to-profit ratios, growth trends, comparisons with other countries. Turn currency and bonds into transparent instruments that reflect real fundamentals.

- **Open Fed Infrastructure to Foreign Banks:**

To counter emerging competitors (like China) that export their financial infrastructure globally, the Fed could offer direct access to U.S. payment rails to select foreign institutions. This cements the U.S. system as a global standard. Currencies matter less if the U.S. controls the "pipes" through which money flows.

- **Infrastructure as the New Currency:**

In a world where traditional currency dominance might wane, controlling or offering superior financial infrastructure could become the main lever of global influence. If the U.S. doesn't adapt, other countries or large private entities might fill the void, reducing the Fed's influence.

This system would prioritize real-time oversight, early intervention, and continuous adaptation, ultimately serving as a global template and ensuring the U.S. remains at the forefront of financial infrastructure and stability.

XIX. A Revolution in Motion: Bridging Finance, Identity, and the Digital Frontier

Imagine a world where sending money across borders is as seamless as sending an email, where your identity is no longer a bureaucratic burden but a tool of empowerment, and where innovation isn't stifled by legacy systems but unleashed by collaboration. This is the promise of the digital revolution in finance—a transformation led by Central Bank Digital Currencies (CBDCs), correspondent banking reinvention[1], and the rise of universal digital identities.

For decades, the financial system has been a complex web of relationships: banks relying on other banks to process transactions, compliance bottlenecks creating costly delays, and entire markets underserved by outdated infrastructure. Correspondent banking[2], once a cornerstone of cross-border trade, has become the **industry's Achilles' heel.** Legacy players like JPMorgan and Deutsche Bank dominate this niche but have little incentive to innovate or extend services to higher-risk sectors. The system is slow, expensive, and rigid—a stark contrast to the agility demanded by today's digital economy.

Enter the untapped potential of correspondent banking for fintechs and emerging markets. Imagine correspondent banking rebuilt from the ground up—a decentralized, horizontal model where banks, fintechs, and even digital wallets are interconnected in two-way corridors. This isn't just a pipe dream. Platforms like BRIDGES are pioneering direct, fully digital correspondent banking networks, integrating compliance[3], core banking, and payment systems into a

---

1. https://l.nansen.id/ChpTkD

2. https://l.nansen.id/yGeYZr

3. https://l.nansen.id/A696ta

seamless experience. The result? Transactions that are not just faster but smarter, with embedded compliance that solves issues before they become problems.

At the heart of this transformation is the promise of Central Bank Digital Currencies (CBDCs). Unlike stablecoins, which rely on private issuers, CBDCs are digital incarnations of state-backed money. They represent the stability of central banks combined with the programmability of digital currencies. For small island nations[4], for instance, CBDCs could democratize access to global financial systems, offering an alternative to reliance on remittances and volatile foreign currencies. These nations, often overlooked, could become testing grounds for innovation, leading the way in adopting blockchain technology and digital identity frameworks.

But what about identity? In the digital age, identity is more than a name or a number—it's the key to unlocking opportunities. Universal digital identities, powered by blockchain and integrated into financial systems, could redefine what it means to "know your customer." They promise to solve the compliance nightmare by making identity verification instantaneous, reliable, and secure. Platforms that embrace this vision are not only rethinking compliance but also addressing the fundamental question of trust in financial systems. After all, compliance is less about separating good actors from bad and more about "following the money"—creating systems that can trace transactions while respecting privacy.

The challenges, of course, are immense. The regulatory landscape is a minefield. Compliance costs for correspondent banks are rising, especially with new regulations like AMLA mandating Know-Your-Customer's-Customer (KYCC) protocols. These costs have driven many legacy players to retreat from the correspondent market altogether, leaving fintechs scrambling to fill the void. Yet, where there are challenges, there are also opportunities. High-risk

---

4. https://l.nansen.id/KcVZls

sectors like cannabis, crypto, and cross-border trade are ripe for disruption. Those who dare to innovate in these spaces stand to reap the rewards.

This revolution isn't just about technology—it's about rethinking the role of financial institutions. Can a bank exist solely as a platform for transactions, without lending or traditional balance sheets? Griffin Bank[5], a pioneer in the UK, has shown that the answer is yes.

---

5. https://l.nansen.id/GTqtXT

Correspondent Banking: A Unique Opportunity for CBDCs and Digital Identity

As we look to the future, the lines between public and private, centralized and decentralized, are blurring. CBDCs and stablecoins, correspondent banks[7] and fintech platforms, regulators and innovators—they are all pieces of the same puzzle. Together, they can create a financial ecosystem that is faster, fairer, and more inclusive. It's a vision of finance where no one is left behind, where identity is a bridge rather than a barrier, and where innovation is not the exception but the rule. This is not just the future of finance. It's the future of trust, the future of opportunity, and the future of us. The question is: Are we ready to embrace it?

Correspondent banking[8], a cornerstone of international finance, is ripe for disruption. While fintech has revolutionized many banking sectors, correspondent banking remains largely untouched, presenting a unique opportunity for innovative technologies like CBDCs and digital identity systems to reshape the future of cross-border payments.

The Untapped Potential of Correspondent Banking with CBDCs: The Future of Cross-Border Payments

Correspondent banking facilitates cross-border transactions by connecting banks worldwide. However, this system is plagued by inefficiencies, including slow processing times, high costs, and complex compliance requirements. These challenges create a significant barrier for businesses and individuals seeking to make international payments, highlighting the need for a more streamlined and cost-effective solution.

Central Bank Digital Currencies (CBDCs) offer the potential to revolutionize correspondent banking. By leveraging blockchain technology, CBDCs can enable faster, cheaper, and more secure cross-border transactions. This could significantly reduce the costs associated with correspondent banking, making it more accessible to businesses and individuals worldwide.

Digital Identity: Enhancing Security and Compliance

Digital identity systems can play a crucial role in enhancing the security and compliance[9] of correspondent banking. By providing a secure and verifiable way to identify and authenticate parties involved in cross-border transactions, digital identity can help mitigate fraud and money laundering risks. This could not only improve the efficiency of correspondent banking but also foster greater trust among participants. Imagine a future where correspondent banking is powered by CBDCs and digital identity. Cross-border transactions would be settled instantly, with reduced fees and enhanced security. Compliance processes would be automated, minimizing delays and errors. This would create a more inclusive[10] and efficient global financial system, empowering businesses and individuals to participate in the global economy with ease. By focusing on compliance-first banking for fintechs and embedded finance platforms, Griffin[11] has challenged the status quo and redefined what it means to be a bank in the digital age.

Correspondent banking is at a crossroads. The challenges of the current system, coupled with the emergence of transformative technologies like CBDCs and digital identity, present a unique opportunity for innovation and growth. By embracing these technologies, we can unlock the true potential of correspondent banking and create a more connected and prosperous world.

XX. IMF 2.0: The SDR Strikes Back in a Multipolar Metaverse

The year is 2035. The IMF's Washington headquarters, once a sedate beehive of beige suits and polite PowerPoints, has morphed into something like a polished e-sports arena for economists. Holographic graphs hover in midair, and staffers pace across glimmering floors discussing liquidity injections the way teenage gamers strategize boss battles. Why the change? Simple: after years of languishing as an arcane artifact, the IMF's Special Drawing Rights (SDRs) are finally back—only this time, they've gone digital and global, streaming in high-definition across central bank dashboards, DeFi pools, and CBDC clearinghouses.

Cambridge's and Oxford's Recent Case Studies

The report authored by my friend, Cambridge's Polina Vertex[1] and her colleagues (Keith Bear[2], Hatim Hussain[3], Hugo Coelho[4] and Bryan Zhang[5]) explores the motivations, approaches, and use cases for Wholesale Central Bank Digital Currencies (**wCBDCs**). This research[6][12] (Download the report)[7] emphasizes wCBDCs as a critical evolution in digital finance, poised to reshape interbank and cross-border settlements while addressing emerging challenges in tokenized asset markets. Here's a summary:

- wCBDCs aim to support digital transaction infrastructures, offering a risk-free settlement asset that mitigates reliance on tokenized private assets like stablecoins or tokenized bank deposits.

- They serve as an alternative to upgrading Real-Time Gross Settlement (RTGS) systems, enabling programmable, always-on, cross-currency liquidity management.

---

1. https://www.linkedin.com/in/pvertex/

2. https://www.linkedin.com/in/keith-bear-2b7407/

3. https://www.linkedin.com/in/hatim-hussain/

4. https://www.linkedin.com/in/hugo-coelho-3ab0a938/

5. https://www.linkedin.com/in/bryanzhengzhang/

6. https://www.jbs.cam.ac.uk/faculty-research/centres/alternative-finance/publications/wholesale-central-bank-digital-currencies/

7. https://www.jbs.cam.ac.uk/wp-content/uploads/2024/12/2024-ccaf-wcbdcs-approaches-implementation-strategies-and-use-cases.pdf

- Tokenized markets are predicted to grow exponentially, with estimates of tokenized asset values reaching $4.6-$5.1 trillion by 2030 (Citibank).

- Increased public-private collaboration to bridge innovation gaps.

- Development of a cohesive definition and regulatory frameworks.

- Balancing innovation with financial system safety and resilience.

In the bustling world of financial innovation, a quiet revolution is taking place—one that has the potential to transform the very fabric of global financial markets. At its heart lies the concept of Wholesale Central Bank Digital Currencies (wCBDCs), a bold initiative championed by central banks to redefine how money flows in an increasingly digitized world. The recent study by Polina Vertex and her team at the Cambridge Centre for Alternative Finance (CCAF) peels back the layers of this emerging phenomenon, revealing a world of possibility, challenges, and collaboration.

Imagine a world where financial transactions are not bound by the rigid structures of today's systems. Instead, picture a dynamic network where cross-border payments occur in real time, seamlessly linking currencies and markets. This is the promise of wCBDCs: a risk-free, digital settlement asset that central banks can wield to anchor the growing world of tokenized assets. From programmable money to atomic settlement (where payment and asset transfers happen instantaneously), wCBDCs are not merely a technological upgrade—they are a vision of what financial markets could be.

Polina[13] and her team take us on a journey through this transformative landscape. They start by addressing the "why" behind wCBDCs. As private innovations like stablecoins and tokenized deposits surge in popularity, central banks face a critical choice: adapt or risk obsolescence. Tokenized markets, estimated to exceed $5 trillion by 2030, demand a settlement system that is just as agile and resilient. The traditional Real-Time Gross Settlement (RTGS) systems—workhorses of interbank payments—may no longer suffice in this always-on, programmable future.

The study doesn't stop at explaining the need—it dives deep into how wCBDCs could work. Across the globe, experiments are already underway. In Europe, central banks have dabbled with Distributed Ledger Technology (DLT) to settle large-scale transactions. The Bank of England's Project Meridian explores ways to synchronize wCBDC and tokenized asset transfers, while the BIS-led mBridge platform is pioneering multi-currency cross-border payments. Each of these efforts reflects a shared realization: the future of money will not be confined to one country or one system.

But the road to wCBDCs is not without its challenges. The Cambridge study highlights the delicate balancing act required. Central banks must ensure that wCBDCs enhance, rather than disrupt, the financial system's stability. Questions abound: Should these digital currencies operate on centralized or decentralized ledgers? Who should control their programmability—central banks or private institutions? And how can global interoperability be ensured without creating a fragmented, "balkanized" landscape?

Despite these hurdles, the excitement surrounding wCBDCs is palpable. For market participants, they represent a bridge to the future—a way to integrate the efficiency and safety of central bank money with the boundless possibilities of tokenization. For central banks, they are a tool to maintain relevance in a world where private money threatens to overshadow public currencies.

Yet, as Polina and her colleagues argue, the true power of wCBDCs lies in collaboration. No single institution can chart this course alone.

Public and private sectors must come together, forging partnerships that blend innovation with regulatory wisdom. It's a call to action for policymakers, technologists, and market leaders to dream boldly while staying grounded in the principles of fairness, security, and financial stability.

This report is more than a technical study—it's a glimpse into the next chapter of monetary history. It challenges us to think big and act decisively. The journey of wCBDCs is just beginning, but one thing is clear: the future of money is not just digital—it is interconnected, programmable, and full of promise. And as we stand at this crossroads, Polina Vertex and her team remind us that the choices we make today will shape the financial world of tomorrow.

In the dynamic intersection of finance and technology, Yuliya Guseva[8] and her co-authors from Rutgers Law School[9], Sangita Gazi[10] and Douglas Eakeley[11], take us on an intellectual journey to explore a new world where public and private money coexist in harmony. Their article, published by the Oxford Business Law[12] "Charting the Co-existence of Stablecoins and Central Bank Digital Currencies[13]," invites us to reimagine the global monetary landscape, blending tradition with innovation.

At its core, money has always been a symbol of trust. For centuries, central banks have issued legal tender to underpin economic stability, while private banks innovated to create diverse financial products. But today, the emergence of digital assets like stablecoins and Central Bank Digital Currencies (CBDCs) is challenging this delicate balance.

---

8. https://www.linkedin.com/in/yuliya-guseva-a2443216/

9. https://www.linkedin.com/company/6123437/

10. https://www.linkedin.com/in/sangita-gazi/

11. https://www.linkedin.com/in/douglaseakeley/

12. https://www.linkedin.com/company/oxford-business-law-blog/

13. https://blogs.law.ox.ac.uk/oblb/blog-post/2024/07/charting-co-existence-stablecoins-and-central-bank-digital-currencies

The authors begin with a critical observation: while central banks provide the bedrock of monetary systems, true innovation often emerges from the private sector. They argue that neither legacy banks nor central banks possess the disruptive agility of fintech pioneers. Legacy institutions cling to established models, and central banks prioritize stability over experimentation. This dynamic creates fertile ground for private innovators like stablecoin issuers to revolutionize payments and settlements.

Stablecoins, these privately issued digital assets pegged to stable values like fiat currencies, offer unique advantages. They facilitate fast, cost-efficient transactions, atomic settlements, and inclusivity in underserved regions. However, their ascent is fraught with challenges. Regulators worry about risks to financial stability, consumer protection, and the sovereignty of central bank policies. Enter CBDCs, which many governments see as a public-sector counterbalance to stablecoins.

But should stablecoins and CBDCs be adversaries? Guseva[14] and her colleagues argue against this binary view. They envision a world where these two forms of money coexist, complementing each other. CBDCs, backed by sovereign trust, could offer unmatched stability and confidence. Stablecoins, on the other hand, bring innovation, user-friendly interfaces, and adaptability to niche market needs. Together, they could bridge the gaps left by legacy systems, fostering financial inclusion and modernizing payment infrastructures.

Yet, coexistence demands thoughtful regulation. The authors advocate for a nuanced, risk-based approach to stablecoin oversight—one that accommodates their diverse business models while addressing systemic risks. They also highlight the importance of interoperability between digital money forms. Through standardized protocols, APIs, and smart contracts, users could seamlessly transition between stablecoins and CBDCs, unlocking the best of both worlds.

The stakes are high. The coexistence of public and private money isn't just a technical challenge—it's a social and economic imperative. Millions remain excluded from traditional financial systems, and outdated payment infrastructures hinder economic growth. By fostering collaboration between public institutions and private innovators, we could build a more inclusive, efficient, and resilient financial ecosystem.

Guseva's essay[15] isn't just an analysis; it's a call to action. She urges policymakers to abandon one-size-fits-all regulatory models and embrace the complexity of digital innovation. The future of money, she suggests, lies not in preserving the status quo but in crafting smarter guardrails that enable growth while safeguarding trust. Ultimately, this article leaves us with a profound question: how can we design a monetary system that marries the stability of public money with the ingenuity of private innovation? The answer lies in a vision of coexistence, where public and private forms of digital money together chart a path toward a more equitable and dynamic financial future.

SDRs: From Dusty Relic to Digital Superstar

Let's be real: SDRs were always the IMF's awkward stepchild—part currency basket, part diplomatic prom queen, yet never invited to the real after-parties of world finance. For decades, SDRs just... sat there, hovering between relevance and irrelevance like a perpetually delayed software update. Pegged to a curated basket of major currencies (the oldies-but-goodies: USD, EUR, GBP, JPY, CNY), they were supposed to be the global reserve asset that everyone loved but no one actually used. The idea: a nice, neutral monetary lingua franca. The reality: a collectible stamp that central bankers tucked away but rarely spent.

Then, someone in the IMF's digital lab had an epiphany: "Why not upgrade SDRs to eSDRs—an encrypted, blockchain-based asset accessible to any central bank with a decent VPN?" And so, the IMF turned the SDR from a relic into a sleek, digital Swiss Army knife for liquidity. Suddenly, eSDRs were zooming around cyberspace, backed not just by currency baskets, but by advanced cryptographic proofs and live transaction ledgers. Central banks could swap them, collateralize them, and park them in global liquidity pools without juggling warehouses of foreign treasuries. The concept of hoarding reserves "just in case" started to feel about as modern as fax machines.

Multilateral Swap Lines 2.0: The IMF's Liquidity Lollipops

The IMF didn't stop at merely digitizing SDRs. Taking a cue from the polyglot language of the internet, they introduced multilateral swap lines facilitated by eSDRs—imagine Google Translate for liquidity. Instead of begging Washington or Beijing for a rescue package, developing nations could now tap into pooled global liquidity, orchestrated by the IMF's servers, and do so faster than a TikTok trend blows up. Stability turned modular. The old fear of "currency wars" and "competitive devaluations" seemed quaint: why fight over which currency rules when everyone can plug into a shared liquidity matrix?

Of course, the big players weren't thrilled. The U.S. grumbled into its bourbon about "loss of dollar dominance," while China smirked, privately delighted that something was finally loosening the greenback's stranglehold. But when every minor currency crisis could be soothed by a quick eSDR injection, the grip of any single hegemon started to slip. Liquidity was no longer a national security asset—it was more like a public utility on the global financial cloud.

BRICS, Baskets, and the Rise of Regional Fintech Superheroes

As the IMF's digital factory churned out its new liquidity potions, the BRICS bloc—Brazil, Russia, India, China, South Africa—took note. "Hey," they said, "if the IMF can do it, why can't we?" Fueled by a mix of ambition and resentment, the BRICS club launched its own stablecoin, a digital asset tied to a basket of their currencies. Think of it as SDR's rebellious cousin who vapes in the school restroom: a currency coalition that bypassed the dollar for everything from soybeans to solar panels. This BRICS Coin didn't just talk the talk; it ran on cross-border blockchains that settled energy transactions between Russia and China in seconds, leaving the old-school correspondent banking system gasping in the dust.

Inspired, other regions followed suit. ASEAN, the African Union, Mercosur—each whipped up its own currency cocktail, sloshing together local mediums of exchange and blending them into something more stable, more digital, and more regionally relevant. The world began to resemble a financial kaleidoscope, each turn of the prism revealing a new cluster of stablecoin alliances. The dollar, once the Iron Throne of global finance, now looked suspiciously like a bulky old armchair no one wanted to lug into their sleek, minimalist apartment.

China's Digital Yuan: The Death Star of the Old System?

Amid this shifting terrain, China's digital yuan loomed large, a fully weaponized CBDC that made traditional correspondent banking feel like carrier pigeons at a drone show. With a quick QR scan, foreign banks could open RMB accounts and tap into a liquidity pipeline that bypassed New York entirely. In development markets from Africa to Latin America, the digital yuan became not just a currency alternative, but a gateway drug to Chinese credit lines, infrastructure loans, and trade deals. It was as if Beijing had built a sleek bullet train station right in your living room, offering you a one-way ticket to a Sino-centric financial galaxy.

Western analysts fretted about debt traps and authoritarian influence. Meanwhile, many developing nations shrugged: "Sure, maybe it's risky, but at least we don't have to beg the IMF for scraps or dance around Fed policy any time we need liquidity." The digital yuan model was sticky, and suddenly the world had more serious questions than whether the next Fed chair would raise rates by 25 basis points.

Tech Giants: Beyond Borders, Beyond Baskets, Beyond Belief

While the IMF and BRICS duked it out in the geopolitical big leagues, the private sector's digital titans were plotting their own financial invasions. Apple flirted with the idea of "iCoin," a stable asset backed by Cupertino's colossal balance sheet. Google teased cross-border stablecoin settlements integrated into its pay platform—imagine emailing money across continents as easily as sending a GIF. Meta tried again, having learned from the Libra fiasco, this time with a stablecoin so deeply integrated into WhatsApp and Instagram that you could pay your friend in Manila just by liking her post. Even Tesla hinted at some cryptic MarsCoin, presumably redeemable for spare rocket parts or EV charge credits.

All of it begged the question: who needs a central bank when you've got the App Store? Governments didn't love this. Some rushed to regulate, others tried to co-opt. But in a world where code is law and networks follow their own gravity, public and private lines blurred. The IMF's once-spartan role now competed with trillion-dollar tech firms and regional alliances that treated currency policy like an open-source software project.

As the dust settled, the global financial system looked less like a neatly ordered hierarchy and more like a decentralized multiplayer game. The IMF's eSDRs provided the global background beat, steady and neutral. BRICS stablecoins remixed the tune for their local dance floors. China's digital yuan choreographed entire cross-border ballets. Tech giants dropped their own remixes, challenging governments to either collaborate or get left behind.

Yet, questions remained: Could the IMF maintain relevance in a space crammed with sovereign contenders and tech juggernauts? Would BRICS stablecoins outlast political squabbles and economic shocks?

Would the world trust Apple or Meta with their life savings? And what if the whole system fragmented into competing digital universes, each with its own rules, incentives, and hidden backdoors?

We don't know yet. But one thing's for sure: the old days of dollar über alles are gone. The SDR, once a half-forgotten footnote in the annals of global finance, now stands at the center of a digital crossroads, smiling ironically as governments, regions, and tech moguls vie for their slice of a frictionless, borderless liquidity dream. Welcome to finance's final frontier. The code is law, the basket is global, and the future is wide open.

XXI. A Blueprint for a Future Beyond the Fossilized Financial Order

I am inviting you to consider an entirely different approach to political program-building—one borrowed from the startup and tech environment. Instead of looking at politics and governance as age-old institutions to be incrementally "improved," we might think of them as dynamic products or platforms that can be reimagined, iterated, and relaunched from scratch when necessary.

Copy Before You Innovate: Reverse Engineering for the Ideal Use Case

In technology, there's a maxim: before trying to outdo Apple, at least learn to replicate simpler, proven models. This is counterintuitive to the political world, where we often expect immediately unique and visionary solutions. By first identifying successful examples of governance—clean, traffic-free neighborhoods, efficient homeless prevention programs, transparent and secure online elections, financially stable pension systems—and directly copying their core mechanics, you build a baseline of functioning services. Only after you've mastered replication should you attempt revolutionary improvements and local adaptations.

This method lowers initial complexity. Rather than conceptualizing a sweeping, never-before-seen overhaul of an entire state, break it down into discrete "features" (like a product's feature list), each sourced from a global best practice. By doing so, you create a modular structure that can be iteratively refined and later innovated upon.

In tech, you don't just iterate linearly—ask what the ideal scenario would look like if there were no constraints. For public services, close your eyes and imagine: instant, fraud-proof elections; zero crime; swift, fair judiciary processes at a fraction of current costs. Don't start from existing institutions and think, "How do we improve this slightly?" Start from the desired end-state and work backward, letting that vision define the changes needed in the "backend" of laws, regulations, training, and infrastructure.

This approach breaks the mental trap of legacy-think. Instead of dragging the heavy baggage of established codes, traditions, and historical paths, you allow the ideal vision to dictate your policy architecture. It's akin to IKEA's approach: first define the customer's maximum price and desired functionality, then challenge designers to build something great within that frame, rather than letting inherited constraints predetermine the outcome.

Embrace the "Technical Debt" Concept and the Clean-Slate Reboot

In software development, starting over is a normal part of the lifecycle. When technical debt accumulates to the point where improvements become too costly or complex, a total rewrite can be the most efficient choice. Governments rarely grant themselves the freedom to do the same. Constitutions, codes, and bureaucratic procedures often feel untouchable because they're "historically rooted."

But what if they aren't sacrosanct? What if you treat a bloated legal code like old, tangled software code—something that can be refactored or even re-launched entirely to fit today's needs? Instead of grudgingly patching old laws and entitlements to accommodate changing realities, leaders could occasionally say, "We're going to rewrite this entire rulebook from a fresh perspective." Tech history shows that such radical resets can unlock new levels of efficiency, clarity, and performance.

Disruptive Innovation as a Political Strategy

Christensen's theory of disruptive innovation suggests that even smart, successful incumbents fail if they cling too tightly to their legacy models. To stay relevant, they must be willing to disrupt their own products, tearing down what worked in the past to create room for what will work in the future.

Translating this to governance: a country might be successful in certain respects but heading toward stagnation or irrelevance if it never dares to rethink its foundational structures. Politicians and public administrators who treat existing institutions as permanent fixtures stifle innovation. Instead, they could encourage a culture where certain governance elements are regularly put "up for grabs," redesigned in sandbox environments, and replaced if the new model tests better. Think of how Jobs revolutionized Apple by distancing himself from the old Apple mindset. Politics could follow suit—envisioning administrations that champion fresh teams (or "skunkworks" projects) tasked with imagining entirely new systems free from legacy constraints.

Political Plans as MVPs and Experiments

Instead of painstakingly trying to develop a comprehensive "master plan" for the entire nation, why not think in terms of MVPs (Minimum Viable Products)? Identify one local service—say, the way building permits are issued—and attempt a radical rework there first. If it succeeds, scale that approach to other municipalities or services. If it fails, learn from it, pivot, and try another approach. Over time, you build a portfolio of successful experiments, each proven on a small scale before being rolled out broadly.

This is the startup method of product development applied to policy: small steps, continuous testing, user (citizen) feedback, and iterative improvement. Rather than guess what works at a macro level, you incrementally assemble a better governance system through a series of well-defined, carefully measured trials.

Expanding "Political Imagination" Through Technology Mindsets

Adopting technology's approach to governance could also reinvigorate citizen interest and participation. When politics are stuck in old paradigms, people tune out. But if politics resemble a dynamic marketplace of evolving services—where new entrants can compete, improvements happen regularly, and citizens get to "test-drive" tangible enhancements—then political engagement could rise. Just as the "democratization" of industries in tech fosters active consumer participation (reviewing, rating, choosing better apps or platforms), so could a more flexible, open-source style of governance reignite civic engagement.

By applying a startup lens to political planning, we can encourage a culture of experimentation, adaptation, and courageous resets. We can learn from global best practices, treat old policies as legacy code ready to be refactored, and always keep an ideal vision in mind. Instead of slowly and painfully trying to improve the old, linear way, we ask: "What does the ideal scenario look like, and how can we engineer backward to achieve it?"

This shift of perspective is not just theoretical—it offers a concrete methodology for rethinking how we build policy, govern states, and engage citizens. It's a way to liberate political imagination from the shackles of tradition and pave the way for more innovative, agile, and responsive forms of public administration.

Applying a "technological approach" to politics and public administration could indeed lead to exciting innovations and increased citizen engagement. Your observations about replicating successful approaches, reverse engineering ideal outcomes, and embracing disruptive innovation are particularly relevant.

From Patchwork to Reinvention

Picture, if you will, a financial world freed from the calcified legacy systems that today dictate every transaction, every currency flow, every subtle shift in market sentiment. Imagine a realm where money, identity, and infrastructure merge into a fluid tapestry of trust, seamlessly woven across borders and platforms—where central banks evolve from inscrutable fortresses into agile orchestrators of a dynamic global economy. In this world, you don't merely tweak the old engine; you strip it down, re-architect it from first principles, and invent something worthy of tomorrow.

The old financial order is like outdated software: layer upon layer of archaic code, "technical debt" accumulated through decades of half-hearted upgrades and regulatory jerry-rigging. Each patch, each workaround, each duct-tape fix builds on a corrupted foundation. In the tech world, we've learned to accept that sometimes you have to start over—tear it down and rewrite from scratch. In public finance, though, there is a stubborn clinging to the old code. Entire legal and economic structures have been duct-taped together by decades of political compromise and historical baggage. Instead of asking how to move forward, we obsess over preserving what we have.

It's time to put that fear to rest. Let's not perpetually "improve" a flawed system with more and more complexity. Let's reimagine. Let's rebuild.

Stablecoins as a Dress Rehearsal: Infrastructure as the New Currency

Consider the stablecoin phenomenon. Yes, stablecoins are often pegged 1:1 to a legacy currency, clinging to the very structures they claim to supersede—thus largely bullshit as an end product. But as a concept, they're illuminating. They prove that it's possible to decouple form from content. Imagine if stablecoins evolved beyond their dollar-pegs into "composite rubrics" referencing multiple currencies—or even baskets of real-world goods and services. That would nudge us away from the mental anchor of the old monetary orders. This is about evolution by substitution: give consumers the shape and interface of money they already know, then gradually shift what's behind it. The "familiar face" of currency becomes a gateway drug to a radically new monetary bloodstream.

We're witnessing the dawn of infrastructure-as-currency. Just as the U.S. dollar once functioned as the global artery for capital flows, tomorrow's financial might will lie in who controls the infrastructure—the payment rails, digital ledgers, cross-border liquidity pipes—on which all other transactions ride. China's CBDC push, for instance, isn't about replacing the dollar with the renminbi through sheer force of currency markets. It's about seizing the plumbing of global liquidity. It's about direct cross-border lending and the ability to shape international financial flows from the ground up. When infrastructure itself becomes the ultimate store of trust and value, national currencies lose their monopoly on monetary imagination.

The Central Bank Autopsy: Unleashing a Wave of Competition

Today's central banks are odd hybrids. The Fed, for example, is a mutation of mandates and historical accidents: part clearinghouse, part lender of last resort, part currency issuer, part regulator—and yet somehow also a bystander to its own complexity. Interwoven with the Treasury, with state-level charters and overlapping authorities, it's a structure so convoluted that clarity and foresight become impossible. We have a currency that's essentially a perpetual deposit (the dollar), while the U.S. Treasury issues bonds—term deposits—that tie the entire system to a bizarre web of maturity transformations and moral hazards.

Let's slice and dice these entanglements into understandable, manageable chunks. Separate the minting function—the actual issuance of currency—from the function of regulating liquidity. Let the "Central Bank" become a transparent platform:

- A Mint/Payment arm that creates and circulates money.

- A Liquidity arm that buys and sells liquidity to maintain balance and stability.

- A regulatory and infrastructure wing that ensures everyone's playing by the same data-driven, real-time rules.

Where does the state fit here? The state, as a borrower, should be just another client in this system—albeit a major one. As a shareholder or founder of the central monetary infrastructure, the state sets high-level policy and direction, but that's different from micro-managing liquidity to benefit its own debt issuance. We must unbundle these roles to remove the opaque incentives and conflicts of interest.

One crucial insight: the U.S. banking sector has grown large, but not strong. It's never learned to compete purely on service and innovation—it's coasted on the back of a booming economy, protected by regulatory complexity and legacy networks. Let's challenge that. Let's drop the barriers and complexities and issue a flurry of new banking licenses. Let's mimic the approach of forward-looking regulators (like the UK or Singapore): encourage a torrent of nimble, specialized "monoline" banks to flood the market with fresh ideas and digital-first services. Force them all to plug into a unified core ledger, a universal core-banking platform provided by the Fed infrastructure so that data flows frictionlessly, compliance is automatic, and consumers benefit from instant and free transfers.

By standardizing the backend and demanding transparency, we zap the system with fresh energy. Real-time dashboards, shared data schemas, and API-first banking will let regulators and citizens see exactly what's going on—no more month-long reporting lags, no more hiding losses until it's too late. In this environment, each bank must truly fight for consumers' trust and attention. The weaker ones fade; the strongest survive and set the tone, pushing continuous improvement across the board.

Embrace the Unknown and Evolve: The Coming Era of Global Financial Competition

We must also revise the regulatory mindset: what's not forbidden should be allowed—at least in a pilot form. Rather than stifling new industries or financial tools, let them run in carefully monitored sandboxes. Learn from the market, gather data, and only then codify rules. This is the opposite of the current stagnant approach. In an era where digital assets, AI-driven credit scoring, and global liquidity platforms sprout like mushrooms after rain, we need regulators who are explorers, not bureaucratic sentinels. As in tech, "learn by doing" must become the mantra for public financial oversight.

Nations are no longer secure behind their capital controls and domestic banking oligopolies. The future is a global bazaar of infrastructural solutions, currency ecosystems, and cross-border liquidity engines. China's CBDC is a harbinger, as are private stablecoins and even corporate-issued debt tokens that start to resemble mini-currencies. If the U.S. Fed and other central banks don't unshackle themselves from legacy codes, others will fill the void. Infrastructure is the new battlefield, and whoever defines the rails defines the game.

The Grand Reset

What I'm proposing sounds radical, even blasphemous: rewrite the financial playbook from the ground up. But why cling to a fossilized order when we have the tools, the knowledge, and the vision to build something better? Global commerce, digital technologies, and citizen expectations have all changed. We're straining against the boundaries of obsolete constructs that assume money and credit must follow 20th-century logic.

If we have the courage to break free—just like a software team decides to refactor its codebase—then we can open the door to a monetary system that is more transparent, more accountable, more competitive, and more ready for the next century. Liberate the central bank from its labyrinth. Turn infrastructure into a service that fosters trust rather than demanding it. Let new players in. Let consumers see the engine in action. Let the entire world see that finance can evolve as freely, as beautifully, as any technology we unleash on the market. The future belongs to those who dare to start again. Our financial system can be that future—if we choose to be its architects rather than its curators.

BANK OF ELON: IMF 2.0

P.S. The Bank of Elon: A Galactic Experiment in Monetary Tomfoolery

Both Zuckerberg and Musk represent a new breed of political influencers – tech billionaires with the resources and platforms to shape public opinion and policy. Their increasing involvement in politics raises important questions about the role of wealth and technology in democracy. While some welcome their contributions, others express concerns about potential biases, conflicts of interest, and the outsized influence they could wield.

Over the past decade, media outlets and analysts have periodically raised the idea that prominent tech CEOs like Mark Zuckerberg and Elon Musk might represent a new breed of political actor, or even consider formal entry into politics. While neither Zuckerberg nor Musk has definitively positioned themselves as traditional candidates in the U.S. political system, the discussions often stem from their public profiles, wealth, and influence on public discourse.

Elon Musk as a Policy Influencer and Public Figure

Musk's penchant for moonshot projects would translate into ambitious infrastructural and exploratory public policies. Expect enormous public works programs to build out hyperloop transport, rapid decarbonization strategies, and multi-national alliances to colonize Mars or build orbital habitats. Musk might turn climate policy into a grand engineering project, leveraging carbon capture at scale, and combine defense and diplomacy with off-world expansion treaties. His governance would almost certainly have a restless, forward-leaning energy—like treating a whole nation (or the planet) as a startup where boldness is rewarded, timelines are tight, and complacency is the enemy.

While Elon Musk has not suggested a run for political office in the same way speculation swirled around Zuckerberg, he's been increasingly seen as a figure shaping public policy discourse:

- **Technocratic Visionary:** Musk's ambition and focus on technological solutions could lead to bold initiatives in areas like infrastructure, energy, and space exploration. He might push for deregulation and prioritize innovation over traditional approaches.

- **Unpredictable Maverick:** His outspoken nature and tendency for unconventional ideas could make him a disruptive and unpredictable force in politics.

- **Political Involvement:** Musk has been much more vocal about his political views, often expressing them on Twitter (now X). He's donated to both parties but has leaned more towards Republicans in recent years. He played a significant role in shaping discussions around the 2024 election and has become a close advisor to Trump.

- **Clegg's Concerns:** Clegg has voiced concerns about Musk potentially becoming a "political puppet master" under Trump, highlighting his "outsized role" in the election and the formation of the new administration.

- **Opinions:** Musk's supporters appreciate his outspokenness and willingness to challenge the status quo. Critics worry about his influence on political discourse, given his massive platform and tendency for controversial statements.

- **Enormous Public Platform:** Musk's frequent use of X (formerly Twitter)—which he now owns—gives him direct access to millions of people and allows him to influence public debates on energy policy, transportation, space exploration, free speech, and AI safety. It's a form of real-time public engagement that many politicians envy.

- **Lobbying and Regulatory Interactions:** Tesla's success rests heavily on government policies related to clean energy and EV tax incentives. Musk's SpaceX similarly operates in close collaboration with NASA and other governmental agencies. His capacity to push, shape, or challenge regulatory frameworks makes him function, in some respects, like a policy entrepreneur, if not a traditional politician.

- **Cultural and Ideological Appeal:** Musk's public persona—touting innovation, risk-taking, and contrarian positions—resonates with certain voter blocs. While he's not a politician, supporters and critics alike often discuss him as though he were a party leader or ideological figurehead, given his outsize influence on public conversation.

- **Political Influence:** Musk has become increasingly vocal on political issues, using his Twitter platform (now X) to express his views and engage with politicians. He has been described as a potential "political puppet master" due to his wealth and influence.

- **Relationship with Trump:** Musk's relationship with Donald Trump has raised eyebrows. He joined Trump's business councils in 2017 but later resigned. More recently, he reinstated Trump's Twitter account and has expressed support for him.

- **Libertarian Stance:** Musk's libertarian views on issues like censorship and regulation have put him at odds with some, including Zuckerberg. His critics worry about his potential influence on policy and the spread of misinformation on Twitter.

If a cohort of tech entrepreneurs—Nick Storonsky (Revolut), Pavel Durov (Telegram), Sam Altman (OpenAI), Elon Musk (Tesla/SpaceX/X), Mark Zuckerberg (Meta), Vitalik Buterin (Ethereum), Balaji Srinivasan (ex-Coinbase/a16z), and Changpeng Zhao (CZ of Binance)—made the leap into politics, we would likely see a dramatic shift in how governance is conceptualized, implemented, and communicated. Their political styles would be shaped by values central to their entrepreneurial careers: a strong belief in technology as a tool for societal improvement, an enthusiasm for rapid iteration and risk-taking, and a global outlook that transcends traditional national boundaries.

This hypothetical future might blur lines between government, commerce, and innovation hubs. It might foreground issues like digital identity, global financial inclusion, decentralized governance, AI policy, and transnational cooperation. However, differences among them—based on their business models, personal philosophies, and cultural backgrounds—would create a politically diverse landscape of "techno-statesmen."

The "New Politician" Concept: Elon Musk's Political Influence

The idea of the "new politician" stems from the recognition that in the digital era, traditional political pathways (coming up through party ranks, holding smaller offices before seeking the presidency) may be challenged by entrepreneurs and tech moguls. These individuals have extraordinary financial resources, massive media platforms, and algorithmic control over information flows. The influence of a platform like Facebook—able to shape public discourse, impact voter turnout, and frame societal issues—gave rise to the notion that its founder was already exercising a form of "soft power" with political consequences. Even without running for office, Zuckerberg's role in moderating global information flows and public debate made him a political figure in all but name.

While Elon Musk never engaged in the same kind of door-to-door handshake tour, he's often discussed in similar terms. Musk's ventures—Tesla, SpaceX, Starlink, Neuralink, and, notably, his ownership of what was formerly Twitter (now X)—place him at critical intersections of policy, infrastructure, and global communications. As a result, journalists and commentators sometimes frame him as operating in a quasi-political role. Through his public statements, online platform moderation policies, and negotiations with governments around environmental regulations, satellite internet provision in conflict zones, and space-launch permissions, Musk wields influence that often surpasses that of many elected officials. He can shape local economies (deciding where to build a Gigafactory), influence energy policy (through Tesla and solar ventures), and insert himself into international affairs (as seen in the Ukraine conflict with Starlink). While Musk cannot run for President of the United States—he was born in South Africa—he has, at times, advocated for or against candidates, engaged in policy debates on social media, and influenced public opinion on a wide range of issues.

- **Background Influence**: Musk's interests in clean energy, space exploration, and digital communication would push frontiers of both domestic and foreign policy.

- **Sustainable Energy & Infrastructure**: Massive investments in renewable energy grids, electric transportation, and hyperloop-like transit.

- **Space Colonization & International Collaboration**: Treating space as a geopolitical frontier—creating policies to collaborate on moon bases, Mars missions, and global space governance.

- **Techno-Futurism & Free Speech**: Balancing platform freedoms with "common sense" moderation, potentially advocating digital "town squares" with less gatekeeping.

- **Governing Style**: Bold, visionary, and prone to making big promises; policies might come with aggressive timelines and a penchant for public spectacle.

Media's Skepticism and the "Techno-Optimist" Mythos

In covering both Zuckerberg and Musk, many outlets express skepticism. They highlight that while these men speak the language of technological progress and innovation, their actual political ideas can be vague, malleable, or driven by corporate interests. There's a tension between their professed commitments to freedom, connectivity, and societal improvement and their profit motives, platform control, and occasional disregard for traditional checks and balances. Observers point out that wielding significant technological and financial power is not the same as having a well-defined political philosophy or the tested political acumen required to govern a country.

Picture this: Mark Zuckerberg already tried waltzing into the financial club with Libra, only to be greeted by an avalanche of dirty looks from the political old guard. The message was clear: "Stick to selling ads and reading our minds through social feeds, pal. Don't you dare touch that shiny money-making printing press called the US dollar." Poor Zuck left with his tail between his legs, stumbling back into the Metaverse to flog VR office meetings no one asked for. A valiant attempt at conquering the monetary frontier, foiled by the guardians of the economic galaxy.

Now, enter Elon Musk. The man who wants to send your grandma to Mars, give your car a personality, and fill Earth's orbit with a million twinkling Starlink satellites so you can tweet cat memes from the Sahara. He's got a track record that would make any politician's knees buckle—SpaceX lands rockets with the casual ease of a gymnast dismounting a balance beam, Tesla profits skyrocket between meme-laden earnings calls, and even Twitter (err, "X") has somehow not imploded despite his best efforts. If anyone can stare down the

Federal Reserve and say "I'm launching my own currency, and it's not just a stablecoin named after a dog," it's Elon.

Add to this unholy concoction one more ingredient: his old buddy Trump. Yes, the same Trump who apparently had him on speed-dial for "special" phone calls at odd hours. If Musk leans into that relationship, we're talking about a potentially unprecedented showdown. The Fed would face a new creature: part tech mogul, part media troll, part rocket scientist, all wrapped in a halo of internet fandom. A single Musk tweet can move markets more reliably than a Fed whisper, so imagine what happens if he spins up "Bank of Elon," fusing the financial system with his already sprawling empire.

Bank of Elon: A Galaxy-Brained Vision

Let's sketch the impossible: The "Bank of Elon," headquartered somewhere appropriately absurd—maybe in a giant glass dome at Starbase, Texas, or aboard a stationary rocket, "for vibes." Instead of mahogany boardrooms, you'd have cryogenic-chilled lounges and a no-shoes policy. The tellers? Chatty AIs that respond to your queries with snarky memes and rocket launch metaphors. And the currency? Let's call it "X-Note," backed not by gold or T-bills, but by Tesla shares, SpaceX's Mars landing schedule, and possibly a smattering of Dogecoin for nostalgia.

This bank wouldn't just do what SVB or any other legacy institution does—no, that's too pedestrian. Instead, it'd integrate finances into every aspect of Elon's ecosystem. Want to buy a Tesla? Finance it directly from Bank of Elon with ultra-long-term zero-interest lines backed by a predicted appreciation in Tesla's machine-learning capabilities. Want to move money abroad? Just beam it via Starlink's secure X-Note protocol—no need for those pesky SWIFT messages. Are you a budding entrepreneur launching a startup on Twitter Spaces? Bank of Elon might issue a "founders' micro-loan" by analyzing your tweet engagement and deciding you're worth a million X-Notes because you made a really good dad joke that morning.

Fed Reserve vs. Musk: Clash of the Eons

How would the Fed respond to this grandiose intrusion into its hallowed turf? Remember, the Fed's existence is predicated on being the serene, grandfatherly figure that nudges interest rates and mumbles economic riddles from a podium. Suddenly, they face a modern PT Barnum who regularly breaks every financial taboo with a grin. The Fed might try to regulate it—maybe they'll issue stern letters, warning that currency issuance is a sovereign right. But Elon could coyly reply, "Cool story, bro," and continue livestreaming rocket engine tests while his digital currency flows through Starlink satellites into every corner of the world.

The Fed once quashed Zuckerberg's Libra attempt by brandishing moral authority and subtle threats. But can they handle Musk's brand of flamboyance? With his electric car empire, he's already captured the climate narrative. With SpaceX, he's got a monopoly on awe-inspiring rocket spectacles. With Starlink, he's built an internet service that can bypass state telecom monopolies. Add a currency to the mix and suddenly he's part central bank, part global ISP, part car dealership. Good luck to the Fed if they think old-school hearings on Capitol Hill can scare him off. He might show up at those hearings wearing a Doge T-shirt and respond to every question with a haiku.

Re-Imagining SVB and the Financial Ecosystem: A New Role for the Dollar—Or Its Demise?

If SVB's fall rattled the system, imagine Bank of Elon as a reinvention of the concept. Instead of panic runs caused by rumors on Twitter, Musk would turn them into publicity stunts. Did the X-Note drop in value because the CEO posted a questionable meme? No problem, we'll just do a flash sale of Starlink subscriptions, capturing new liquidity from all over the world. The volatility that kills normal banks could be a feature for Elon's empire—every crisis an opportunity to show off how flexible and "anti-fragile" his financial architecture is.

Most importantly, Musk might push the idea that the Fed's slow, backward-looking approach is for dinosaurs. He might broadcast a vision of a dynamic currency and banking system that updates in real-time—responsive to machine learning algorithms and rocket launch schedules. "Who needs quarterly Fed meetings to set rates when we can let our currency's interest be pegged to the cadence of SpaceX missions to the Moon?" he'd say, eyes sparkling with mischievous glee.

A successful Bank of Elon wouldn't necessarily kill the dollar. But it might force the dollar to shapeshift, learn new tricks, and come out of its comfort zone. Suddenly, the greenback has competition: a private "cosmic" currency with the PR panache of an influencer, integrated into a tech ecosystem touching transport, communications, and energy. The Fed might have to raise its game, perhaps finally investing in a slick digital currency solution or forging alliances with other central banks to counter Musk's gravitational pull.

Or maybe Musk, in a dramatic, meme-worthy gesture, could proclaim that the Bank of Elon's ultimate goal isn't to destroy the Fed, but to "liberate" it. He might say: "The Fed can become a platform, an open API for global liquidity—just like I made Tesla's patents open-source!"

Of course, this would send every central banker into cardiac arrest, but at least it's a conversation starter. Let's be real: Most likely, regulators, politicians, and assorted financial guardians would unite to contain Musk's monetary ambitions before they get too wild. But the very notion that a tech mogul could even try—and possibly get somewhat far—says a lot about the times we live in.

The Grand Theatre of Modern Finance: 'Electra' vs 'Libra' - Money as Votes

So, cue the dramatic music. The stage is set for an epic showdown between a centuries-old institution wearing pinstripes and a self-styled techno-visionary wearing a T-shirt and tweeting from a Mars-bound rocket. If Zuck's Libra attempt was a warning shot, Musk's Bank of Elon could be the full-on rocket barrage. Will he reimagine the role of SVB and the Fed, turning the world's financial systems into just another playground for his ambitions? We'll have to wait for the next livestream. Just make sure you have a bag of popcorn—and maybe a few X-Notes handy to tip the cameraman.

What is The Next Big Startup for Elon Musk? Imagine a startup called [1]"**Electra**"[2] —a secure, online voting platform designed to bring the full election process into the digital age. (Or - "**Civimetr**"? - is a secure, KYC-based online voting platform designed to streamline and modernize elections at all levels—local, regional, and national.) Its core vision is to offer a turnkey solution for organizing and holding elections at any level—district, city, regional, or national—while drastically reducing cost, improving transparency, and increasing voter turnout. Essentially, it's the infrastructure that could turn a referendum or a mayoral election into a matter of just a few clicks, all with the rigor and security of a well-run financial transaction system.

- **KYC-Verified Voters:**

    Every participant on Electra's platform undergoes a secure Know Your Customer (KYC) process—similar to opening a

---

1. https://medium.com/@slavasolodkiy_67243/electra-online-voting-platform-designed-to-bring-the-full-election-process-into-the-digital-age-e4c53b989e75
2. https://medium.com/@slavasolodkiy_67243/electra-online-voting-platform-designed-to-bring-the-full-election-process-into-the-digital-age-e4c53b989e75

bank account or registering for secure online services. This ensures that each ballot is cast by a unique, verified individual, eliminating fraud and double voting. KYC could be handled via partnerships with trusted identity verification providers, biometric verification (e.g., face scan + government ID), or state-issued digital identities where available.

- **Transparent, Auditable Architecture:**

Counting votes becomes fully transparent with real-time dashboards. Election officials, observers, and even voters (to a certain extent) can audit the tally. Electra could employ blockchain or other distributed ledger technology to ensure an immutable record of votes and recounts at any time, making "hanging chads" or suspicious USB drives with voting machine data a relic of the past.

- **Election "Blueprint" Library (The Constructor):**

To handle the diversity of election types and legal frameworks, Electra maintains a dynamic "constructor" or template library. This database contains predefined templates for different election models—first-past-the-post, ranked-choice, proportional representation, runoffs, referendums, etc. Administrators from a municipality or a country simply select their governance model and apply it, cutting down on custom engineering work for each new election.

Over time, as Electra integrates more electoral rules from various countries and jurisdictions, setting up a new election in line with local laws becomes as easy as selecting options from a menu.

- **Unit-Based Rollout Strategy:**

Rather than trying to convince a major Western democracy to overhaul their electoral system overnight, Electra targets small, low-stakes, and less affluent municipalities first—places that can't afford expensive traditional elections. By starting small (maybe a rural county council, a small island municipality, or a poor region that struggles with printing ballots and manual counting), Electra can demonstrate how quickly and cheaply an election can be run online.

Let's pick a small municipality in a developing country that's open to innovation—maybe a community election for a school board or a local council. They run their election via Electra: voters receive a secure link, log in with their verified identity, and cast their votes from home or a community center's computers. Results are known within hours after polls close. Costs are minimal—no printed ballots, no lengthy manual counts.

https://chng.it/LzChmFKvQ5

This first successful unit serves as the MVP that proves the concept's viability. Electra documents metrics: how much money was saved vs. a paper-based election, how quickly results were delivered, and how voters perceived the transparency and fairness. Then Electra[16] takes this data to investors and larger jurisdictions.

- **Scalable Unit Economics:**

  After the first pilot, Electra refines the cost model. Initial setup (R&D, platform architecture, security audits) is expensive, but once those costs are sunk, running additional elections becomes cheaper—marginal costs plummet. Pricing might follow a tiered subscription model: a small council election costs a few hundred dollars, while a nationwide election could cost thousands or millions, but still far less than a traditional election infrastructure.

To ensure a path to profitability and scale, Electra can also offer add-on services:

- **Analytics & Insights:** Detailed voter engagement analytics for political parties and election commissions.

- **Candidate & Campaign Tools:** A parallel platform where candidates can set up official profiles, host Q&A sessions with verified constituents, and present their platforms (monetized as a premium service).

- **Consulting & Legal Integration:** Services to help integrate Electra's system into existing legal frameworks, including training for officials.

Over time, as Electra accumulates a customer base of election commissions, political organizations, and even corporate boards (for internal votes), the recurring revenue builds.

- **High-Turnout and Convenience:**

One major selling point is the potential to improve turnout. By letting people vote securely from their phones or home computers, Electra removes friction—no travel to polling stations, no weather issues, no long lines. This convenience could dramatically increase participation, which can be tracked and showcased as a major success metric. Early adopters—municipalities that want to increase civic engagement—become case studies.

- **Environmental and Cost Efficiency:**

Marketing collateral emphasizes how many tons of paper ballots and how much gasoline for transporting ballot boxes and election staff are saved per election. This narrative appeals to environmentally conscious regions and can attract NGOs or foundations that promote sustainable governance.

- **Security and Trust Building:**

Trust is the linchpin. Electra invests heavily in cybersecurity—penetration tests, bug bounty programs, compliance with international standards (e.g., ISO 27001), and real-time monitoring against hacking attempts. Partnerships with reputable cybersecurity firms and possibly academic institutions lend credibility. Electra might even run "shadow elections" parallel to official ones for demonstration and integrity comparison. In authoritarian contexts, it could offer external oversight groups secure, third-party verification of poll results, potentially becoming a tool for democratic validation.

- **Legal and Political Navigation:**

Some countries have stringent laws that don't allow online voting. Early focus might be on referendums or non-binding consultation votes to demonstrate feasibility. Over time, as trust is built and success stories accumulate, legislative changes might follow, making online voting a legal option. The startup can help governments draft modernization bills or partner with international organizations that recommend best practices in digital democracy.

- **Global "Election Design" Consultancy:**

Beyond technology, Electra can offer an "Election Designer" service—experts who help tailor the platform to local electoral laws, simplify ballot design, and even advise on fair voting methodologies. This is another revenue stream and adds value beyond just the tech platform.

In the long run, the startup becomes a global standard for digital elections, reducing overhead costs, waste, fraud, and inefficiency. Turnout improves because voting becomes as easy as logging into your secure account. Counting and announcing results happens in real-time, under global scrutiny. By building a robust ecosystem of templates and services, Electra simplifies and streamlines the entire electoral process worldwide—just as online banking did for finance or e-commerce did for retail.

- **Stage 1 (MVP & Pilot):**

Launch in a small municipality (maybe 5,000 voters) to run a local council election. Prove reliability, reduce cost drastically, publish a case study.

- **Stage 2 (Scaling Within a Region):**

Approach a set of 10–20 municipalities in neighboring regions or countries with similar governance structures. Offer discounts for multi-jurisdictional adoption, build brand recognition, refine user experience and KYC process.

- **Stage 3 (Vertical Expansion):**

Move beyond government elections to include other institutions that hold votes—unions, corporate boards, shareholders' meetings. This vertical diversification ensures stable cash flow and continuous platform use beyond public election cycles.

- **Stage 4 (International Recognition):**

Once credibility is established, target more developed or mid-sized cities in stable democracies looking to experiment with online referendums or pilot e-voting in off-season elections. Begin integration with legal frameworks. Garner endorsements from international election monitoring bodies.

- **Stage 5 (Global Marketplace for Elections):**

With a large library of election types and best practices, position Electra as the go-to platform for quickly organizing any kind of vote—public, private, national, local, or organizational. Continuously improve security, scalability, and user experience.

It's a moonshot, but the blueprint is rooted in practical MVP thinking: start small, solve one municipality's election problem perfectly, document success, then expand step-by-step—unit by unit, election by election. What do you think, Elon?)

BANK OF ELON: IMF 2.0

https://l.Nansen.id/**bookEng** https://l.Nansen.id/**AIjustice**

https://l.Nansen.id/**NavalnyCardAPPLE**

---

[1] https://www.linkedin.com/in/johnsinclairfoley/

[2] https://www.ft.com/content/d43e9743-f376-4a18-8fc3-c3b9f1867425

[3] https://www.theinformation.com/articles/larry-summers-has-a-message-for-silicon-valley

[4] https://www.youtube.com/watch?v=7b6D9exbsA[3]

[5] https://l.Nansen.id/Summers

[6] https://en.wikipedia.org/wiki/Full-reserve_banking

[7] https://l.Nansen.id/ChpTkD[4]

[8] https://l.Nansen.id/yGeYZr[5]

[9] https://l.Nansen.id/A696ta[6]

[10] https://l.Nansen.id/KcVZls[7]

[11] https://l.Nansen.id/GTqtXT[8]

[12] https://www.jbs.cam.ac.uk/faculty-research/centres/alternative-finance/publications/wholesale-central-bank-digital-currencies/

[13] https://www.linkedin.com/in/pvertex/

[14] https://www.linkedin.com/in/yuliya-guseva-a2443216/

[15] https://blogs.law.ox.ac.uk/oblb/blog-post/2024/07/charting-co-existence-stablecoins-and-central-bank-digital-currencies

[16] https://medium.com/@slavasolodkiy_67243/electra-online-voting-platform-designed-to-bring-the-full-election-process-into-the-digital-age-e4c53b989e75

---

3. https://www.youtube.com/watch?v=7b6D9exbsAc

4. https://l.nansen.id/ChpTkD

5. https://l.nansen.id/yGeYZr

6. https://l.nansen.id/A696ta

7. https://l.nansen.id/KcVZls

8. https://l.nansen.id/GTqtXT

www.ingramcontent.com/pod-product-compliance
Ingram Content Group UK Ltd.
Pitfield, Milton Keynes, MK11 3LW, UK
UKHW042019040225
454602UK00016B/364